Three Studies in 20th Century
Obscurity

FRANCIS RUSSELL

Three Studies in Twentieth Century Obscurity

HASKELL HOUSE
Publishers of Scholarly Books
NEW YORK
1966

HASKELL HOUSE PUBLISHERS Ltd.

Publishers of Scarce Scholarly Books

280 LAFAYETTE STREET

NEW YORK, N. Y. 10012

Russell, Francis, 1910–
   Three studies in twentieth century obscurity.   New York
Haskell House, 1966.

   124 p.   22 cm.

   Reprint of the 1954 ed.
   Bibliographical footnotes.

   CONTENTS.—Joyce and Alexandria.—Kafka.—Gertrude Stein.

   1. Joyce, James, 1882–1941.   2. Kafka, Franz, 1883–1924.   3. Stein,
Gertrude, 1874–1946.   I. Title.   II. Title: Twentieth century
obscurity.

   PR6019.O9Z79   1966   68–658
, ISBN 0-8383-0678-0

   Library of Congress   [5]

Printed in the United States of America

CONTENTS

Joyce and Alexandria - - - - 7

Kafka - - - - - - - - 45

Gertrude Stein - - - - - 66

Acknowledgements - - - - - 123

JOYCE AND ALEXANDRIA

IT is a generation now since the publication of *Ulysses*, more than a decade after Joyce's death, and yet though most of the literary dust that he stirred up in his life has subsided, his significance in the history of our time is still unclear. For the average reader he remains the impressive but unread author of *Ulysses*, for his detractors he is as Dr. Gogarty once called him, the anti-pope of literature, for his partisans he stands beyond time, a colossus with cosmic attributes. In his unpublished letter to *The Times* after Joyce's death, T. S. Eliot, who had given Joyce the accolade of Classicist, summed up the uncertainty of the literary era of which he and Joyce had been two of the pontiffs. 'To some of Joyce's younger contemporaries, like myself', he wrote, '*Ulysses* still seems the most considerable work of imagination in English in our time. . . . I do not believe that posterity will be able to controvert this judgement, though it may be able to demonstrate the relative insignificance of the literary achievement of the whole period.'

Finnegans Wake, with its contrived artifact language that goes far beyond *Ulysses* in the disintegration of normal speech, is held by coterie critics to be the apocalyptic culmination of Joyce's work. Eugene Jolas, who published successive fragments of *Finnegans Wake* as *Work in Progress*, asserted in regard to it that 'when the beginnings of this new age are seen in perspective it will be found that the disintegration of

7

words, and their subsequent reconstruction on other planes, constitute some of the most important acts of our epoch'.[1]

A recent volume on Joyce, in a series dealing with the influential thinkers of the last hundred years, places him on a level with Darwin, Einstein, Freud and Marx. Yet, but for the world notoriety of what *The Pink 'Un* called 'The Scandal of Ulysses', *Finnegans Wake* would have found neither publisher nor readers, and Joyce's work would be as forgotten today as that of the lesser contributors to *The Yellow Book*. As Herbert Gorman later said, the effect of the publication of *Ulysses* in 1922 was like dynamite in the literary world. Analyzing the phenomenon, critics have failed to note its inevitability. *Ulysses*, whatever its other claims, stands out as the classic of revolt in the intellectual climate of the post-war period. By the logic of events it or something similar to it was bound to be written. If it had appeared fifteen years earlier it would have been uncomprehended, while fifteen years later it would have lost much of its sting and become almost commonplace. As it was, *Ulysses* exactly fitted the repudiating Zeitgeist of the 'twenties.

The artist in revolt is often closer to his Hegelian time-spirit than is the artist who accepts the weight of tradition. Professor Lowes in *Convention and Revolt in Poetry* limited his study to formal verse, but what he has written of poetry applies equally to all the arts: 'Revolt in poetry is not a wind that blows aloof and fitfully along the upper reaches of the air. It is bound up with the general ebb and flow of attractions and

[1] Our Exagmination round his Factification for the Incamination of 'Work in Progress' (Paris, 1929), p. 79.

repulsions which go to make up life. And it is never amiss to begin by scrutinizing life, when one is questioning the ways of poetry.'[1]

The artist, the inventor and the scientist are equally sensitive to the intellectual ferment of their times; each is able to extract what he needs from it for his particular task, to sense the potentiality of the future and by so doing to help bring about its actualization in the present. In the field of applied mechanics Thomas Edison invented, among other things, the electric light and the phonograph. Yet, when he was young, such devices were floating in a kind of collective time-consciousness, invisible but just around the corner. If Edison had never lived, some one else before long would have contrived the incandescent lamp and some spatial method of recording sound. Two generations before the Hitler epoch Nietzsche sensed that ominous shadow. It is no belittling Einstein's genius to say that if he had not evolved his theory of relativity some one else would have done so by this time.

So it was with *Ulysses* in 1922. In the transvaluations brought about by the 1914-18 cataclysm its effects would inevitably be felt in the literary world. There is always a time-lag between the evolution of scientific and philosophic theories and their somewhat less exact application to literature. Freud and Bergson as part of the intellectual current of the twentieth century had not yet had a full-bodied literary incarnation. Under their influence, in a decade of self-conscious dis-

[1] (Constable, 1919), p. 159. See Dr. Jung's *Ulysses: A Monologue* (Zurich, 1934). p. 12. 'Like every true prophet, the artist is the unwitting mouthpiece of his time through whom it tells the secrets of its soul, and he is sometimes as unconscious as a sleepwalker. He supposes that it is he who speaks, but the spirit of the age is his prompter.'

illusionment, somebody was certain to write a book in defiance of the traditions of the established world of letters that would reflect the psychological theories of the Viennese school, and use the stream of consciousness technique. Such a book, exploring the non-logical roots of consciousness, would almost by necessity affront the current language taboos.

The Anglo-Saxon monosyllables to describe the excretory and sexual functions of the body are still used generally in common speech, although they fell out of polite use and written form with the introduction of the language of Latin-derived substitutes. We find some of them occurring in Chaucer, one at least in the Authorized Version, in disemvowelled form in the seventeenth and eighteenth centuries, and they were completely banned only with the rise of the bourgeoisie in the Victorian era. This censorship persisted, though weakened, through the first two decades of the twentieth century—Joyce himself found his use of the word 'bloody' taken exception to in *Dubliners* in 1912. Eventually it would be challenged in the post-war period. As it happened the challenge was made by two authors of very different intent, D. H. Lawrence who in *Lady Chatterley's Lover* made a puritanical effort to remove the salacious connotations of the monosyllables and restore them to their pre-conquest innocence, and Joyce in *Ulysses* who used the banned forms with a detachment that did not quite succeed in avoiding self-consciousness.

The sexual episodes and the use of the monosyllables in the bewildering uncomprehended bulk of *Ulysses* set off the scandal. Not since *Jude the Obscure* had there been such an outcry against a book, and a comparison of the two is an indication of how the literary atmosphere had changed within Hardy's overlapping lifetime. Today, when the barriers between colloquial and literary speech are much less well-defined, when *Ulysses* is on the reserve shelves of most women's colleges and Joyce exegesis has become a vested interest, it is difficult to apprehend that violent mood of the early 'twenties when the book for awhile seemed to have become all things to all men. The established world of letters, uneasy in an era of change and fearing for the accepted scale of values, felt with Shane Leslie that *Ulysses* was a kind of literary Bolshevism. Alfred Noyes found it 'the foulest book that has found its way into print'. Paul Elmer More viewed it with antiseptic disgust. For Edmund Gosse, Joyce's writings were 'worthless and impudent . . . a perfectly cynical appeal to sheer indecency'.

By the older professors in the universities Joyce was scarcely ever mentioned, but to the younger men, restive under the shadow of a tradition no longer vital for them, *Ulysses* was a welcome explosive to demolish the fusty academic structure. The book became a potent means of challenging the genteel tradition. It was, according to the Joyce cult that quickly grew up, a Bible and Koran for all would-be writers. Joyce was the master stylist of the English language in whom all the styles of the past coalesced and English literary history culminated. *Ulysses* became the shibboleth of the New Freedom.

It was more than a book, it was a movement. Among his partisans Joyce early assumed the messianic rôle he himself claimed. From the time he reached maturity he had had no real existence outside his writing. The significant part of his life ended on June 16th, 1904, the day in which the action of Ulysses takes place and which he celebrated as an anniversary in after years. Standing outside contemporary life, like Balzac his characters became more real to him than real people. Unlike Balzac he confused the Byzantine intricacies of his technique with the primal act of creation. According to Stuart Gilbert, who wrote his commentary on *Ulysses* in collaboration with Joyce and who reflected Joyce's own opinion, '*Ulysses* is a book of life, the life of a microcosm which is a small-scale replica of the universe, and the methods which lead to an understanding of the latter will provide a solution of the obscurities in *Ulysses*'.[1] Why or how an understanding of *Ulysses* would bring us closer to the enigma of the universe is never explained. It is pronounced like a fiat. Later on Mr. Gilbert compares *Ulysses* to a 'great net let down from heaven including in the infinite variety of its take the magnificent and the petty, the holy and the obscene, inter-related, mutually symbolic. ... In this banal day in the life of an inglorious Dubliner, we may discover an entire synthesis of the macrocosm and a compelling symbol of the history of the race'.[2] For Mr. Gilbert, as for the coterie round Joyce at the time, the flat assertion seemed sufficient proof of its truth. Elsewhere Mr. Gilbert speaks of Joyce as 'viewing the Cosmos with the eye of God'. S. Foster Damon in his article in *The Hound and Horn*[3] identified the Mr. Bloom of *Ulysses* with Christ and Joyce-Daedalus with Satan, an identification that delighted Joyce who when he left Ireland as an unknown young

[1] *James Joyce's 'Ulysses'* (Faber & Faber, 1930), p. 39.
[2] ibid, pp. 45-7.
[3] *The Odyssey in Dublin* (*The Hound and Horn*, Vol.III, No. 1, Autumn, 1929).

man dramatized himself romantically as Lucifer, the son of morning. Marcel Brion states in *Our Exagmination of 'Work in Progress'* that 'in *Ulysses* and still more in *Work in Progress* we seem to be present at the birth of a world.'[1] Robert Sage claims for Joyce's writings that 'he has embraced the world, heaven, hell and the celestial bodies. . . . He has telescoped time, space, all humanity and the universe of gods and heroes.'[2]

In the seventeen-year interval between the publication of *Ulysses* and *Finnegans Wake* Joyce had become academically respectable, no longer Lucifer trailing fire, but a mandarin of the contemporary literary scene, his name familiar even to the many who had not read his books. There was something old-fashioned, slightly pathetic about those who still challenged his position. *Finnegans Wake*, however, caused no such scandal as *Ulysses*. The latter shocked by its bluntness of expression, the former bewildered. As Joyce in *Ulysses* tried to weave together the myriad threads of a single Dublin day, so in *Finnegans Wake* he attempted to encompass the dream-unity of a Dublin publican during a night's sleep. *Finnegans Wake* is written in an artificial language intended to reproduce the vague fitfully-conscious world of dreams. Because of its rejection of conventional English speech—a process foreshadowed in *Ulysses*, but carried on here even to the tentative disintegration of the alphabet—the book was not comprehensible except to the initiate. It seemed at first a more poetic version of Esperanto, richer in tone, with echoes of music and onomatopoetic associations, but lacking Esperanto's logical

[1] op. cit. p. 29.
[2] ibid., p. 55.

syntax. During the previous decade parts of it had appeared in *Transition* accompanied by various commentaries and elucidations that owed most of their substance to verbal hints from the author. Edmund Wilson, in his essay on *Finnegans Wake*, admitted that without the explanations offered in *Transition* it would be doubtful if anyone could get the hang of the book. *Work in Progress*, like a tantalizing enigma, kept Joyce in the eye of the intellectual public. *Finnegans Wake* after a decade of pre-publication gossip became the most advertised book in advance since *Nana*.

Doughty, after *Arabia Deserta* appeared, was accused of using the English language as if he had found it lying around loose. Joyce used it as if he were reconstituting the shattered glass of a mediaeval cathedral, often with dazzling colour and effect, but with the old formal pattern lost. Mr. Wilson describes this language as consisting of 'words and sentences which, though they seem to be gibberish or nonsense from the rational point of view, betray by their telescopings of words and their combinations of ideas, the involuntary preoccupations of the sleeper.'[1]

If *Ulysses* was a scandal, *Finnegans Wake* was a mystification. Its portmanteau words, gleanings from a dozen languages, and strange syllabic combinations rising up like hippogryphs through the pages, were grafted onto the structure of a minor baroque philosopher's doctrine of eternal recurrence plus a Nordic mythus contrived by Joyce himself. To the unprepared layman first picking up the book it seemed to resemble one of those freak publications that from time to time are printed by wealthy schizophrenics. Joyce's brother

[1] *The Wound and the Bow* (W. H. Allen & Co.), p. 259.

Stanislaus, who had shared the earlier years of his brother's exile in Trieste, returned his gift copy as a gesture of protest. Nevertheless *Finnegans Wake* was a richer field for exegesis even than *Ulysses*. What Joyce's readers lost in mass they gained in intensity. The claims for this last book were even more cosmic than for *Ulysses*, and Joyce the author became increasingly identified with a creator possessing divine attributes.

To Joyce's followers he was the Logos. Samuel Beckett in *Our Exagmination of 'Work in Progress'* made the high claim that 'Joyce's writing is not *about* something; it is that something itself.'[1] A reviewer in the *New English Review* considered *Finnegans Wake* the most important work since the last great religious books. He went on to assert that 'if anyone were to imagine the language which the dead speak when stirred or troubled, their drowsy talk would resemble the words used in *Finnegans Wake*. Words echoing with many meanings, visionary revelations, profane experiences, and dark magic; they often seem to come from beyond the edges of earthly life. . . . This clown's book which teaches us to descend the comic steps into hell, where Christ's truth is hidden, requires that sad and wise understanding of what is tragic and outside history.'[2]

Two research workers, Joseph Campbell and Henry Morton Robinson, spent the war years in fashioning a key to *Finnegans Wake*, and their study—almost as long as the original—contains both a running commentary and paraphrasings into conventional English. Later scholiasts have claimed that the Campbell-Robinson

[1] op. cit., p. 14.
[2] Vol. XV, No. 4, October, 1947.

work is a misinterpretation. However, although suffering from the authors' lack of a first-hand knowledge of Ireland, it is probably as long and painstaking a work as will be produced on the subject. If it is inaccurate it will be hard to expect accuracy anywhere. *Finnegans Wake* may eventually draw forth as many commentaries as certain end products of the Alexandrian school, but there will never be a fixed canon.

For Messrs. Campbell and Robinson *Finnegans Wake* is 'a kind of terminal moraine in which lie buried all the myths, programmes, slogans, hopes, prayers, tools, educational theories, and theological bric-a-brac of the past millenium.'[1]

Whatever its value as interpretation, *A Skeleton Key to Finnegans Wake* is a summing up of the various deific claims made for Joyce. 'What, finally, is *Finnegans Wake* all about?' Messrs. Campbell and Robinson ask. And their answer is: 'Stripping away its accidental features, the book may be said to be all compact of mutually supplementary antagonisms: male-and-female, age-and-youth, life-and-death, love-and-hate; these, by their attractions, conflicts, repulsions, supply the solar energies that spin the universe. . . . James Joyce presents, develops, amplifies and recondenses nothing more or less than the eternal dynamic implicit in birth, conflict, death and resurrection.'[2]

In *A Skeleton Key*, as in so much Joyce criticism, we find again the ex cathedra pronouncements: 'Besides being a Dream Confessional, *Finnegans Wake* is also a Treasury of Myth. Myths, like dreams, are an up-working of the unconscious mind—and Western

[1] *A Skeleton Key to Finnegans Wake* (Faber & Faber, 1947), Introduction.
[2] ibid., p. 14.

scholarship has recently become aware of their essential homogeneity throughout the world. *Finnegans Wake* is the first literary instance of myth utilization on a universal scale. Other writers—Dante, Bunyan, Goethe —employed mythological symbolism, but their images were drawn from the reservoirs of the West. *Finnegans Wake* has tapped the universal sea.'[1]

Mr. Campbell, contributing to a later compilation of essays on Joyce, sees *Finnegans Wake* as a sealed revelation containing 'a prodigious anonymity of feeling, indifferent alike to vice and virtue. A readiness to permit not only civilizations, but the universe, galaxies of universes, to be generated and annihilated in the wheeling rounds of time, is the sign of the apocalypse of this transhumanistic biologico-astronomical revelation.'[2]

The extraordinary value placed on *Ulysses* and *Finnegans Wake* by an originally small circle of critics and the later wide acceptance of such far-reaching claims among intellectuals is as significant for the era as for the books themselves. Whatever one's feelings as to Joyce's permanent literary value, he holds an important place in the cultural history of our time. Writing of *Ulysses*, Harry Levin, in perhaps the most balanced study of Joyce to date, aptly summed this up: 'The immediate qualities which make it (*Ulysses*) so poignant an expression of the modern mind, for most readers, are chaos, dissonance and obscurity.'[3] Why these particular qualities should appeal to the contemporary time-spirit cannot be answered finally within the same cultural period.

[1] *A Skeleton Key to Finnegans Wake*, p. 361.
[2] *James Joyce: Two Decades of Criticism* (Vanguard, 1948), p. 370.
[3] *James Joyce* (Faber & Faber, 1941), p. 370.

2

Indeed, such a question is only formulated at that stage of a culture when it becomes introspective and uncertain of itself, when literary production tends to become increasingly hermetic, and esoteric criticism to flourish. In this connection Dr. Freud's references to originality in science are equally pertinent to literature. 'Many interesting comments', he writes, 'may be made about what appears to be scientific originality. When, for instance, a new idea appears in science, that is, an idea which is at first considered new and, as a rule, attacked as such, an objective research soon proves that it is not really so novel. Usually, the discovery has already been made, repeatedly, often at periods far apart, and has fallen into oblivion.'[1]

Although they may be superficially altered by the accidents of geography and language, literary movements tend basically to repeat themselves within similar cultural periods. It is not possible to determine with any exactitude why chaos, dissonance and obscurity draw so much emotional response from the modern mind. Most of the reasons given are rationalizations, but we can at least examine past eras that bear a resemblance to our own. Perhaps the closest parallel with the intellectual atmosphere since the end of the first World War is to be found in Alexandria of the third century B.C. There the same triad of chaos, dissonance and obscurity flourished within the limits of the clique about the Alexandrian Library. It is true that Theocritus, the greatest poet of that self-absorbed age, stood outside the coteries, but he was a pastoral anachronism. More typical of the period was Callimachus, an enigmatic but genuine poet who could at

[1] *Collected Writings.* Vol. XL, p. 295.

times capture the music of incantation as well as Theocritus, yet who for the most part occupied himself with the intricate narration of esoteric legends in what Professor Wright has called a desperate desire to be original. Then there were lesser and more wilfully obscure poets like Dosiadas and Euphorion who founded schools of criticism on the basis of their pedantry. Of all the Alexandrian coterie poets the most enigmatic was Lycophron, who was called even by his contemporaries σκοτεινὸς, the dark one. In his surviving work, the *Alexandra*, one finds a startling parallel with the later work of Joyce, from the assumption of the pseudo-epic form to the use of a fabricated language.

Alexandria in the age of Lycophron was the greatest commercial city in the world, a metropolis of culture superseding the small Greek city-states, sophisticated, urbane, detached, and at the same time permeated with inner doubt. The bonds of the older Greek tradition had been broken, but the end result was enervation rather than freedom. Art became eclectic and the artist, free to borrow from the Egyptian, the Asiatic or the Minoan according to his taste, found himself increasingly hampered by frustration and impotence. It was a period of dissolving beliefs and shifting standards, as Charles Kingsley called it, 'a generation of innumerable court poets, artificial epigrammists, artificial idyllists, artificial dramatists and epicists; above all a generation of critics.'[1]

Literary movements followed each other in waves, one moment at their crest, the next shattered on the beach. Characteristic of all these movements however

[1] See Kingsley's essay, *Alexandria and her Schools*.

was their remoteness from the general public. Their glyptic lines and involved thought-patterns were not intended for those who liked the simple music of Homer. The poets of this period formed an exclusive society writing for each other and for a limited group of cultured amateurs. Each coterie praised itself and attacked its predecessors. There were symbolists, enigmatists, superrealists, pattern poets who wrote verses on the objects described—such as a shepherd's pipe or an egg. Religion and patriotism had become too archaic as subject matter; the epic involved insuperable difficulties. Poets for the most part could no longer sustain a long theme. They preferred epigrams or the brief epic-inspired poems called Epyllion.

As poetry became unreadable except for the Library clique the general public took to light reading, books not unlike the best sellers of the present, as well as simplified outlines of science and history. Poets like Euphorion and Lycophron found themselves increasingly restive within the limitations of the language they had inherited, and to extend the last subtle essence of their meaning they began to break down the inner structure of language and reform it after some inner pattern of their own. The cliques approved. For to understand these poets at all was to set oneself apart as a cultural initiate. As Professor Couat explained: 'No initiation is without its mystery; the Alexandrian poets like to have their meaning guessed at rather than understood; they do not surrender the key to their erudite language at first reading ; occasionally we recognize them by the very fact that they are unintelligible.'[1]

[1] *Alexandrian Poetry under the First Three Ptolemies* (Paris, 1882), p. 136.

The great distinction of the Alexandrian age, its permanent contribution, was in the fields of mathematics and science. It was the age of specialists, of Euclidean geometry, of spectacular advances in medicine and astronomy. Such abstruse sciences, demanding a life-time of concentrated application, were without influence on poetry. The poets, from what they considered their higher sphere of vision, looked down on such men as Euclid and Archimedes. Just as between poetry and practical life, the divorce between science and poetry was complete, and poetry thrown back on itself began to eat its own words.

Lycophron, because he expresses the tendencies of the Alexandrian school in their most extreme form, and because his *Alexandra* through its stubborn obscurity has survived, is the most representative literary figure of the period. Like Joyce he is a focal point of his age. Just as much of Joyce's work that has found response in our era will be incomprehensible to future periods, so the effect that Lycophron had on his contemporaries is lost to us. We know that he did have such an effect, we have the enigmatic bulk of the *Alexandra* to prove it to us. But we know little of his life. Joyce's we know in detail. If we knew more of Lycophron we could no doubt trace his life sequence in his work, just as we can in Joyce; and as the end result was similar we might expect the pattern of both men to be roughly the same.

The pattern of Joyce's life is an arithmetic progression from simplicity to a heavily shadowed multiplicity. In his early twenties he composed the transparent obvious verses of *Chamber Music*, pretty conventional *fin-de-siècle* rhymes such as a young member of the Rhymers' Club might have written. *Chamber Music* is the type of thin little book that many a young man of talent writes and has privately printed, and often writes no more. But Joyce, with that intransigeant egocentricity that is characteristic of many artists and most characteristic of him, claimed them to be the greatest lyrics since Shakespeare. He intended to conquer Dublin with his rhymes. In revolt against his poverty, his appalling family life, his Jansenistic religious background and his lack of recognition—although he had as yet done nothing to merit the latter—he felt he had been cheated of his birthright, the birthright of that still elegant upper-middle-class ascendency society whose image he was to recreate in the home environment of his later Parisian years.

George Moore, referred to ironically by Joyce as a 'genuine gent', was able to leave Ireland and work in London without bitterness. He felt too sure of his position in the world to question his surroundings. Joyce, when he first left Ireland for only half a year, saw himself as an outcast, an exile. The pose of exile was his favourite form of self-dramatization; it was the title of his Ibsenesque play in which he expressed his wish-fulfilments more directly and naïvely than in anything else he wrote. From Zurich, after he had left Ireland for the second time with the woman who twenty years later was to become his wife, he sent back to his Dublin acquaintances a bitter doggerel poem, *The Holy Office*, in which he visualized himself as Byron's Cain:

> I stand the self-doomed, unafraid,
> Unfellowed, friendless and alone,

Indifferent as the herring bone,
Firm as the mountain ridges where
I flash my antlers on the air . . .
And though they spurn me from their door
My soul shall spurn them evermore.

No doubt if Joyce had been born of an Irish county
family of wealth and position he would not have felt
the same inner compulsion to revolt. In an article on
Joyce and psychoanalytic theory, Frederick J. Hoff-
mann noted the 'very striking correspondence between
Joyce's shift to literary experiment and his spiritual
renunciation of his earlier tradition.'[1]

Joyce's first prose work, the collection of short
stories he called *Dubliners* and which he characteristi-
cally announced as 'a chapter in the moral history of my
country', are slight but acute sketches of no great
depth, written in a traditional manner. In a letter to the
publisher, Grant Richards, Joyce explained that he had
written the stories in a 'style of scrupulous meanness'.
Professor Levin has referred to them as 'the annals of
frustration'. They are bitter vignettes, written without
heart and without much feeling, except for the last
story. This story, *The Dead*, alien in mood to the rest,
Joyce wrote some time after the others. It has a com-
passion, a sympathetic almost tender understanding
that one does not find elsewhere in Joyce. Although
marred by its purplish ending, it leaves one with a
sense of wondering pity. Written without emphasis on
technique, it is a moving indication of what Joyce
might have become if he had developed within the
limits of conventional language.

[1] *James Joyce: Two Decades of Criticism,* op. cit. p. 403

There is a well-known passage in Joyce's revised autobiography, *A Portrait of the Artist as a Young Man*, apparently an excerpt from his diary written shortly before his first trip to Paris, where he speaks of making his way using only the weapons at his command—silence, exile and cunning. 'I go', he wrote, 'to encounter for the millionth time the reality of experience and to forge within my soul the uncreated conscience of my race.' As yet he had written nothing but *Chamber Music*. He was full of the hot resentment of a young man who believes passionately in himself and who has not yet developed the means to convince others. What he meant by this rhapsodic language was that he now intended to write the autobiography which exists in fragmentary form today as *Stephen Hero*. The uncreated conscience was no more than a foreshadowing of one of those autobiographical novels in which the Werther-ish figure of a sensitive young man emerges from an unhappy childhood to a defiant adolescence and finally realizes his artistic mission when he leaves in the last chapter to write the book that the reader has just concluded. The 300,000 words of *Stephen Hero*, later to appear in a much modified and more mature form as *A Portrait of the Artist as a Young Man*, were what Joyce was to forge. If *Stephen Hero* had been promptly accepted by any of the twenty publishers who rejected it, if *Dubliners* or even *Chamber Music* had been acclaimed in Dublin, if Joyce had found himself famous overnight like the young Kipling, he might have made his peace with Ireland. When his first child was born in Trieste in 1905 he sent his father a mocking telegram: 'Son born. Mother and bastard doing well.' But, for all his bitterness, he was back in Dublin seven years later for the third time, dickering with Maunsel & Company who had agreed and were now reluctant to publish *Dubliners*. At thirty, approaching middle age, Joyce was still willing to accept Dublin, if Dublin would have him.

But Dublin would not. Maunsel's, after what must have been to Joyce agonizing delays, refused to publish *Dubliners* and destroyed the proofs. With that gesture all hope of reconciliation ended. Joyce abandoned and repudiated Ireland, the polite literary world and all that went with it. He had been rejected, and he would answer rejection with final defiance. Although *Dubliners* and the revised version of Joyce's autobiography were not to appear for another two years, his life course was now determined. As Herbert Gorman noted in his semi-official biography of Joyce: 'His failure in Dublin had intensified the bitterness he felt towards that city and its inhabitants. He was convinced that a conspiracy to crush him completely existed amongst his former companions.'[1] How he pictured himself at that period is clearly shown in his play, *Exiles*, where one of the characters melodramatically addresses the emigré writer, Richard Rowan—obviously Joyce himself: 'You have that fierce indignation which lacerated the heart of Swift. You have fallen from a higher world, Richard, and you are filled with fierce indignation when you find that life is cowardly or ignoble.'

Joyce's fiercest indignation was caused by the fact that he was not readily accepted at his own valuation. Years later, when *Ulysses* had made him famous and *Work in Progress* was appearing in brief extracts, an American critic asked him if he did not make too heavy

[1] *James Joyce* (Farrar & Rinehart, 1939), p. 219.

demands on his readers. Joyce's reply was that the demand he made of his readers was that they should devote the whole of their lives to reading his works. That uncompromising assertion is again characteristic.

Dr. Gogarty, smarting from his gross portrayal in *Ulysses*, called Joyce the Great Repudiator. He did repudiate all that bound him to a mean and hateful and dogmatic past—country, church and literary tradition—but he was to find that the past, even when repudiated, still dominated his life. The present never greatly concerned him after he left Ireland, and though he was to live away almost thirty years, his past there was still the one reality for him. Although his work would develop in astonishingly new paths, he himself remained rooted emotionally in Edwardian Dublin.

Joyce's first five books up to the publication of *Ulysses* are merely prolegomena. *Chamber Music* and *Stephen Hero* are obvious enough, *Exiles* though revealing is incidental. With *Dubliners*, however, one finds Joyce taking the first step in the strange process that was to end in the convolutions of *Finnegans Wake*. In these short stories the syntax is clear but the plot withers away; there is mood rather than meaning. With *A Portrait of the Artist as a Young Man*, Joyce has commenced tentatively to experiment with language, and one finds the beginnings of that disintegration in syntax that in *Ulysses* is to be carried to such lengths. In the latter work sentences and sentence structure break away, subjective and objective impressions fade into each other, syntax is shattered. If words still retain their form, with a few onomatopoetic exceptions, they alone survive. In *Finnegans Wake* the disintegration is complete; words have lost their old identity, dissolving and recombining as strange hybrids. There is even a beginning of the disintegration of the alphabet—a process afterwards carried to much greater extremes by Joyce's friend Ezra Pound in *The Pisan Cantos*.

August, 1914, found Joyce at work on the book that was to make him known to the world, a task he was to continue with monomaniac concentration for seven years, oblivious to the tragedy of the war, feeding on his own bitterness as he quarried the unwieldy bulk of *Ulysses* out of the past. The defiant impulse that protested so thinly in *The Holy Office* had now found form and substance. *Ulysses* is, as Cyril Connolly said, still a young man's book, 'packed with the defeatism and guilt of youth, its loneliness, cynicism, pedantry and outburst of bawdy anarchic activity.'[1] But in its expression the author has attained his angry maturity. Gilbert Seldes called it an epic of defeat. Professor Levin saw in the epic parallel a complete lack of the epic virtues of love, friendship and magnanimity.

Fortunately for Joyce's literary reputation his own inner nihilism corresponded with the outer nihilism of his age. *Ulysses* is the full-bodied expression of an anti-philosophy, and the instinctive understanding of this by Joyce's contemporaries accounts for much of the book's impact. Curtius called it Luciferan, a work of the Anti-Christ, and maintained as did Dr. Jung that a metaphysical void lay at the root of Joyce's work. Professor Levin saw no heavenly nets descending nor the secrets of the macrocosm suddenly revealed. 'A student', he wrote, 'who demands a philosophy from

[1] *The New Statesman and Nation*, Vol. XXI, No. 517, January 18, 1941.

Joyce will be put off with an inarticulate noise and a shrug.'[1]

Whatever Joyce's adaptation of myths and the use of the Viconian theory in his later works, he himself had no beliefs. He once remarked to Eugene Jolas that we know nothing and never shall know anything. For Joyce the universe was an impenetrable mystery ruled by blind chance, and human life had no purpose. There was neither God nor any rational substitute for God. At the same time Joyce had the impelling emotional need to assert himself, and as he had nothing else to cling to in a shifting universe he clung to the unalterability of past time. Like Proust he became obsessed with the past as the only fixed quality of existence.

Much of *Ulysses* is wilfully obscure, as if Joyce had turned his hatred of bourgeois Ireland and his years of poverty to a scorn of the reader; much is dull and pedantic, but for all its faults it is still a tremendous book. There are parts of it in which Joyce comes close to succeeding in the impossible task of recapturing a vanished day.

Just as Joyce's books are a progression from clarity to obscurity, so one finds the same sequence within *Ulysses* itself. The first three chapters are an exposition in which Joyce employs the stream of consciousness technique as a bridge between the mental and physical world. Such a technique, after its novelty wears off, can become one of the dullest means of expression known, but Joyce uses it with surprising success. There is a supple dynamic strength to the movement of those opening pages. One sees as an almost tangible mental image the actuality of that

[1] *James Joyce*, op. cit., p. 74.

summer morning in 1904, the fog-streaked air over the glaucous waters of Dublin Bay, the mailboat leaving the Kingston pier with the smoke from her funnel wisping out in the direction of Howth Head, oyster catchers and herring gulls perched along the sandbars, and the shimmer and glitter of the reflected sunlight on the old Martello tower as Buck Mulligan struts along the parapet, the breeze ruffling his dressing gown. From this opening chapter dominated by Mulligan's boisterous and jocose vulgarity to the chapters on Stephen Daedalus's walk along Sandycove Beach and Paddy Dignam's funeral as it makes its way through the long-vanished viceregal Dublin, one feels that Joyce has successfully conjured up the phantom of the past.

Joyce's basic device of using the *Odyssey* as a parallel gives him an integrated framework within which he can arrange his material, and as such it is successful. The failure of *Ulysses* comes with Joyce's egocentric pedantry that pushed parallels to such bizarre extremes that the work became a vast mosaic of conflicting symbols. According to Mr. Gilbert, 'each episode of *Ulysses* has its Scene and Hour of the Day, is (with the exception of the first three episodes) associated with a given Organ of the human body, relates to a certain Art, has its appropriate Symbol and specific Technique. Each episode has also a title, corresponding to a personage or episode of the *Odyssey*. Certain episodes have also their appropriate colour.'[1]

Such verbal by-plays add to the mystification of the reader, but it is difficult to see what else they accomplish either in depth of understanding or clarification.

[1] *James Joyce's 'Ulysses'*, op. cit., p. 27.

It is of little advantage to the reader to know that the paragraph before him reproduces the peristaltic action of the stomach, that several pages of words juxtaposed apparently without order or sequence mimic the effects of musical notation, or that a long chapter on the birth of a child is written in the parodied styles of several dozen authors to illustrate the evolution of the English language from the womb of Anglo-Saxon. *Ulysses* as it continues loses its clearness and becomes a web spun by stubborn egotism and woven by unbalanced pedantry.

Joyce has, as several critics have noted, combined the two diverse currents of naturalism and symbolism, but the combination is not a synthesis. Throughout *Ulysses* he strikes off bright sparks of naturalism that glow and flicker out in the brackish waters of his symbolist obsession. Many fragments and partial episodes are successful—the Gertie MacDowell interlude written in the circulating library style of the 'nineties, Father Conmee's walk, bathos used as an effective medium in the far too prolonged incident in the cabman's shelter. Much of the Walpurgisnacht scene in the brothel is brilliant, but again Joyce mars the effect with his relentless piling up of fantastic detail and his lack of balance. Mrs. Bloom's soliloquy is a remarkable *tour de force*, though the lucubrations of a somewhat promiscuous lower-middle-class Dublin housewife are scarcely what Joyce maintained them to be, 'the voice of Gaea-Tellus, the Great Mother speaking . . . the goddess whom the Romans invoked by sinking their arms downward to the earth.'[1]

Joyce's ground plan of *Ulysses* is as involved as a

[1] *James Joyce's 'Ulysses'*, p. 19.

Swiss calendar watch, and as in the latter, use is lost sight of in ingenuity. Just as he compared his first lyrics with those of Shakespeare, so in *Ulysses* he placed himself on a level with Homer and the source of all poetry. Mr. Gilbert expresses Joyce's Luciferan self-esteem when he announces that 'James Joyce is, in fact, in the line of classical tradition that begins with Homer; like his precursors he subjects his work, for all its wild vitality and seeming disorder, to a rule of formal discipline as severe as that of the Greek dramatists; indeed the "unities" of *Ulysses* go far beyond the classic triad, they are manifold and withal symmetrical as the daedal network of nerves and blood streams which pervade the living organism.'[1]

In *Ulysses* and even more in *Finnegans Wake* Joyce did in fact create a most elaborate pseudo-mytho-logical crossword puzzle to which only he could ever furnish the complete key. From his basic disbelief he somehow assumed in his word-games semi-divine qualities. Like Lycophron in Alexandria, by evolving his own mythus and his means of expression he succeeded in creating a baffling mock-epic, a learned conundrum for scholiasts to explore.

In spite of the obscurities of *Ulysses* its bitterness is evident enough. Joyce in his seven years' labour had managed among other things to pay off the old scores of two decades. Now between the blue covers of his finally published book he took his revenge on all those who had crossed him, from Dr. Gogarty and his other Dublin acquaintances to an obstinate and obscure British Consulate official Joyce met in Zurich a dozen years later. The 'Kartharsis-Purgative' he had

[1] *James Joyce's 'Ulysses'*, p. 30.

vainly asserted in *The Holy Office* he found at last in *Ulysses*.

At the age of forty he had achieved the position in the world that he had demanded at twenty. He had attained recognition, a fame tinged with notoriety, and, through the generosity of a woman admirer, what was no less important—financial independence. Savage introspection no longer lacerated his heart. In his flat in a fashionable quarter of Paris he surrounded himself with old family portraits, those estimable evidences of continuity so dear to the Anglo-Irish ascendancy. When Cyril Connolly visited him during the 'twenties he almost always found Joyce wearing the white blazer and gold-threaded crest of an obscure Dublin cricket club he had belonged to as a young man. He enjoyed the long-deferred luxury of living the kind of life he felt was due to him, which, according to Mr. Connolly, was 'that of a well-to-do high priest of art, remote from equals and competitors, and not too accessible to admirers.'[1]

On finishing *Ulysses* Joyce was faced with the common artistic problem of what to do next. By writing the most complex novel of his day, by breaking with the customary rules of exposition, syntax and logic, he had placed himself outside the bounds of conventional criticism. Neither the detractors nor the admirers of *Ulysses* could apply the usual standards to it. For the former the book became a manifesto of anarchy and for the latter a new revelation. If Joyce, after *Ulysses*, had retreated to the inherited clarity of *A Portrait of the Artist as a Young Man* the hostile critics would have fallen on him. To retain his

[1] *The New Statesman and Nation*, op. cit.

Olympian position above criticism his only course was to stay beyond criticism. From *Ulysses* he moved on to the gigantic anagram that is *Finnegans Wake*.

For seventeen years he spent his time elaborating that many-layered labyrinth, creating both myth and language in the process. The myth, unlike the *Ulysses* parallel, was a cosmic one of his own contriving, based roughly on Vico's doctrine of recurrence. As Professor Levin explained it: 'Anagogically, it envisages nothing less than the development of civilization, according to Vico's conceptions. Allegorically, it celebrates the topography and atmosphere of the city of Dublin and its environs. Literally it recalls the misadventures—or other nightmares of H. C. Earwicker . . . Morally it fuses all these symbols into a central theme—the problem of evil, of original sin.'[1]

According to the *Skeleton Key* interpretation 'Finnegan the hod carrier is identifiable first with Finn MacCool, captain for two hundred years of Ireland's warrior heroes, and most famous of Dublin's early giants. Finn typifies all heroes—Thor, Prometheus, Osiris, Christ, the Buddha—in whose life and through whose inspiration the race lives. It is by Finn's coming again (Finn-again)—in other words by the reappearance of the hero—that strength and hope are provided for mankind.'[2] At the close of their gradus Messrs. Campbell and Robinson explain the Joycean technique: 'Joyce . . . became dissatisfied with the one-dimensional declarative sentence and conventional vocabulary. Pioneer and transinsular spirit, he could not repose contentedly within the bounds of experi-

---

[1] *James Joyce*, op. cit., p. 157.
[2] *A Skeleton Key to Finnegans Wake*, op. cit., p. 4.

ence and expression delimited by the Anglo-Saxon tongue. . . . With a greed unmatched in the history of Literature he seized all language for his province. He had sucked Latin in with the milk of his Jesuit education; with Greek, Sanscrit, Gaelic, and Russian, he was on terms of scholarly intimacy. He spoke Italian in his own home; French and German were second mother tongues to him. Obscure dialects, argots, the slang of many nations clung to his ear like limpets. As a young man he had learned Norwegian in order to study Ibsen; oddments from Finnish, Arabic, Malay, Persian and Hindustani are plentifully sprinkled through *Finnegans Wake*. . . . Not content with this traffic in staple words, Joyce hangs numberless outriggers of association on every syllable.'[1]

Mr. Wilson, tracing through one layer of Joyce's associations, saw Earwicker as 'Tristram stealing Iseult, yes; but—at the suggestion of an Adam's mantlepiece in the bedroom where he is sleeping— he is also Adam, who has forfeited by his sin the Paradise of Phoenix Park; at the suggestion of a copy of Raphael's picture of Michael subduing Satan which hangs on the bedroom wall, he is an archangel wrestling with the Devil. And he has fallen not merely as Adam but also as Humpty Dumpty (he is fat and his first name is Humphrey); as the hero of the ballad of *Finnegans Wake* who fell off a scaffold while building a house (but came back again at the sound of the word "whisky"); and as Napoleon (an obelisk dedicated to Wellington is a feature of the Phoenix Park; and there is apparently a Wellington Museum). Since the landmarks of the life of Swift still keep their prestige in

[1] *A Skeleton Key to Finnegans Wake,* p. 358.

Dublin, he is Swift', etc.[1] William Troy saw Earwicker as 'Adam-Caedmon, the original and perfect man, from whose dismembered body have come the multiple phenomena of the earth.'[2]

All these threads and many more can be traced through *Finnegans Wake*. Joyce used a polymyth structure where one discovers everything from Adam to Humpty Dumpty, where rivers and landscapes are personified and language dissolves. The Viconian cycle itself was merely a convenient scaffolding. It is difficult to imagine that Joyce really believed in Vico's four succeeding phases of theocracy, aristocracy, democracy and finally chaos, this last phase to be terminated by a clap of thunder by means of which an awed and terrified mankind would be driven back to its original theocracy. Vico's thunder appears in *Finnegans Wake* onomatopoetically several times in words of 100 letters, as at the beginning, 'bababadalgharaghtakam-minarronnkonnbronntonnerronntuonnthunntrovarrh-ownawnskawntoohoohoordenenthurnuk!'[3] Like the book as a whole it gives Joyce a rare chance to play with syllables, but it is no duplication of the thunder's reality any more than Joyce's complete logograph with its arbitrary and multiple references is a history of mankind.

Joyce was a connoisseur of etymology, who collected words the way other men collect stamps or minerals. After the success of *Ulysses* he gave himself up completely to his hobby and with his own natural bent to intricate enumeration built up the Babel tower of *Finnegans Wake*. The reader may well ask, dismayed at

[1] *The Wound and the Bow*, op. cit., p. 247.
[2] *James Joyce: Two Decades of Criticism*, op. cit., p. 314.
[3] *Finnegans Wake* (Faber & Faber, 1939), p. 3.

the farrago of words and at the assertion that he should spend the rest of his life pondering over this complex book, what strange, new and overwhelming doctrine lies beneath all this cosmic machinery, what is the stupendous truth that has to be expressed in a new language of compounded words? Professor Levin begs the question by maintaining that what we do not understand we at least feel. 'We are borne from one page to the next, not by the expository current of the prose, but by the harmonic relations of the language—phonetic, syntactic, or referential, as the case may be.'[1] Dr. Jung said of *Ulysses* that behind a thousand veils nothing lay hidden. In *Ulysses*, however, there was the naturalistic element, and Joyce's positive force of hate and defiance. In *Finnegans Wake* Joyce reached a serenity and a detachment new to him. The lean years were over. He was at peace with himself at last, and writing for his own intellectual amusement. Basically though he had nothing more to write about. At the core of his elaborate word-pyramid was an empty room.

One can take almost any random passage from *Finnegans Wake* and by puzzling over it for some time find enough simple associations of the compound words to reduce the passage to some sense and order, even as one can, at first try, fill a certain number of squares in a crossword puzzle. As such it can be amusing, but has no more philosophic value than any other kind of conundrum. According to Messrs. Campbell and Robinson, the following passage, a birth image, represents 'the coming into being of Homo sapiens at the close of the ice ages, or of Western Man

[1] *James Joyce*, op. cit., p. 184.

after the fall of Rome; it represents, too, the birth of
the individual after the night of the womb, and the
dawn of ego-consciousness,'[1]

'But however 'twas 'tis sure for one thing, what
sherif Toragh voucherfors and mapqiq makes put out,
that the man, Hume the Cheapner, Esc., overseen as
we thought him, yet a worthy of the naym, came at this
timecoloured place where we live in our paroqial
fermanent one tide on another, with a bumrush in a
hull of a wherry, the twin turbin dhow, *The Bey for
Dybbling*, this archipelago's first visiting schooner, with
a wicklowpattern waxenwench at her prow for a figure-
head, the deadsea dugong updipdripping from his
depths, and has been repreaching himself like a fish-
mummer these siktyten years ever since, his shebi by
his shide, adi and aid, growing hoarish under his
turban and changing cane sugar into sethulose starch
(Tuttut's cess to him!) as also that, batin the bulkihood
he bloats about when innebbiated, our old offender was
humile, commune and ensectuous from his nature,
which you may gauge after the bynames was put uder
him, in lashons of languages, (honnein suit and praisers
be!) and totalising him, even hamissim of himashim
that he, sober serious, he is ee and no counter he who
will ultimendly respunchable for the hubbub caused in
Edenborough.'[2]

The authors of *A Skeleton Key* do not divulge how
they were able to discover so much in a single fluid
sentence, but even if it were as they have stated, it is
hard to see what is gained by such elaborate conceal-
ment. The fact is that beneath the subterfuges,

[1] *A Skeleton Key to Finnegans Wake*, op. cit., p. 55.
[2] *Finnegans Wake*, p. 29.

beneath the word-play—that can at times be pleasantly musical as in Joyce's recorded readings from the Annalivia Plurabelle passage—no vital thought exists. In the end Joyce's only message to us is that he has none.

Oddly enough the most coherent passages in *Finnegans Wake*, those that follow the course of conventional English most closely, are autobiographical, coming from the random thoughts of Shem the son of Earwicker—otherwise James Joyce himself.

From the security of his mandarin position Joyce looked back with a tolerant smile at the pride of his insolent young manhood, and at his angry challenging self of only yesterday defiantly at work on *Ulysses* in some fly-blown back room. He even poked fun at the book that had made him famous, his 'usylessly unreadable Blue Book of Eccles', as he called it, punning on the title and the blue cover of the original Paris edition of *Ulysses*, the name of Eccles Street where Mr. Bloom lived, and an early Irish manuscript, the *Yellow Book of Lecan*. Of himself as the author of *Ulysses* he wrote: 'He scrabbled and scratched and scribbled and skrevened nameless shamelessness about everybody he ever met.'[1] *Ulysses* he called 'an epical forged cheque on the public for his private profit.'[2] A few pages on there is an amusing reference to Joyce's final departure from Ireland after Maunsel's publishing house—encountered here as 'Robber and Mumsell, the pulpic dictators'—had destroyed the proofs of *Dubliners*. 'He winged away on a wildgoup's chase across the Kathartic ocean and made synthetic

---

[1] *Finnegans Wake*, p. 182.
[2] ibid, p. 181.

ink and sensitive paper for his own end out of his wit's waste.'[1] Looking back on the haughty 'Non serviam' declaration of his youth, Shem-Joyce remarks to himself, 'You have reared your disunited kingdom on the vacuum of your own most intensely doubtful soul. Do you hold yourself for some god in manger, Shehohem, that you will neither serve nor let serve, pray nor let pray?'[2]

Joyce mocked himself equally with his work. 'Neither of those clean little cherubum Nero or Nobookisonester himself, ever nursed such a spoiled opinion of his monstrous marvellosity as did this mental and moral defective.'[3] 'Who can say how many pseudostylistic stamiana, how few or how many of the most venerated public impostures, how very many piously forged palimpsests slipped in the first place by this morbid process from his pelagiarist pen?'[4]

Joyce did not even spare the book he was working on from his veiled ridicule. He became Maistre Sheames de la Plume, who would if his 'lankalivline lasted wipe alley English spooker, multaphoniaksically spuking, off the face of the erse[5] . . . unconsciously explaining, for inkstands, with a meticulosity bordering on the insane, the various meanings of all the different foreign parts of speech he misused and cuttlefishing every lie un-shrinkable about all the other people in the story, leaving out, of course, foreconsciously, the simple worf and plague and poison they had cornered him about until there was not a snoozer among them but

[1] *Finnegans Wake*, p. 185.
[2] ibid, p. 188.
[3] ibid, p. 177.
[4] ibid, p. 182.
[5] ibid, p. 178.

was utterly undeceived in the heel of the red by the recital of the rigmarole.'[1]

Joyce in his seventeen years' labour took almost microscopic pains with his fantastic structure. In the Anna Livia Plurabelle episode he wove together a patchwork of the names of 500 world rivers, and in the Alexandrian elaboration of those few pages he told a critic he had spent over 800 hours.

As he neared the end of his last book his mood seemed to change from the detachment of myth and language to a personal melancholy. The sorrow of his private life began to weigh on him increasingly, no longer centred in himself but this time in the tragic development of his two children. His father's death in 1931 affected him deeply in spite of all their early differences. Beyond *Finnegans Wake* there is no indication that he had any further literary plans. Through the now lessening distortions of its last pages one senses this undercurrent of regret and unfulfilment. Ostensibly the voice is that of the River Liffey flowing through Dublin and losing itself finally in the sea, but behind the feminine disguise it is Joyce the travel-wearied aged man speaking: 'But I'm loothing them that's here and all I lothe. Loonely in me loneness. For all their faults. I am passing out. O bitter ending: I'll slip away before they're up. They'll never see. Nor know. Nor miss me.'[2]

If we know much about Joyce's life, we know little of Lycophron's. He was born some time before 300 B.C. and became an early exile from his native Chalcis, arriving as an unknown young man in Alexandria

[1] *Finnegans Wake,* pp. 173-4.
[2] ibid, p. 627.

during the reign of Ptolemy Philadelphus. A few years after his arrival he came under the patronage of the Court and was appointed to the Alexandrian Library. There in conjunction with his official duties he wrote an exhaustive study of the works of the comic poets. He moved in the intellectual circles of the city, became one of the Pleiad, a now forgotten group of seven tragic poets who produced experimental plays, and according to Ovid died on the stage while playing a rôle in one of them. He himself composed over forty plays, none of which have come down to us.

Lycophron survives in the history of Greek literature only as the author of the *Alexandra*, its most enigmatic and undecipherable production. In the Alexandrian age he seemed as significant to the scholastics of the Library as Joyce has done to present-day critics. However, in the *Alexandra*, the disguised cross-references to contemporary events, the neologisms and word-play, the many-layered mythological parallels, restricted it to a small cultural élite of contemporary aesthetes and intellectuals who though they considered Lycophron of transcendent importance· were unable to transmit any of his significance to posterity. Professor Wright in her *History of Greek Literature* called the *Alexandra* 'a monument of learned folly, the labyrinth of Lycophron "the obscure", composed for an academic clique and interesting to that clique alone.'[1]

The *Alexandra*—another name for Cassandra, the daughter of Priam—is a long poem in tragic iambics, a monologue spoken by the slave who was set to watch

[1] Wilmer Cave Wright, *A Short History of Greek Literature* (American Book Co., 1907), p. 445.

Cassandra and report her prophecies to the King. These prophecies extend from the Fall of Troy to the Alexandrian present, and through their network of mythological and antiquarian erudition there are veiled allusive comments on contemporary events. One finds references to Roman conquests, and a surviving fragment of exegesis explains the lion that plays an uncertain role in the latter portion of the poem as Alexander the Great.

Lycophron deliberately misled his readers. He used private key epithets recurringly throughout the *Alexandra*. He was apparently obsessed with esoteric place-names. Whatever action there is in the poem dissolves in anagrams, puns, paraphrases, foreign words, portmanteau nouns and a coined vocabulary. A third of the words Lycophron used were of his own invention, being found nowhere else in Greek literature. He combined disparate phrases, borrowed from Asian dialects, twisted archaisms into new forms. As patterns for his mythologue he tore old myths to pieces and patched together their fragments. The arid pseudo-epic that he evolved made him known through its very difficulty of comprehension. According to M. Croiset, interpreting Lycophron became a professional feat for ancient commentators. 'Yet', M. Croiset maintains, 'in this unbearable poetry, one must recognize that there was technical cleverness and even the germ of an idea.'[1]

Whatever eschatological secret Lycophron in his hermetic passages may have seemed to hold for the circle of initiates in Alexandria, is lost to us. His pseudo-epic has been passed down and survives by

[1] Alfred Croiset, *A History of Greek Literature* (Paris, 1899), p. 460.

reason of its baffling obscurity as a sterile freak of literature, accidentally immortal through its monumental emptiness, when the greater number of plays of Aeschylus, Sophocles and Euripides are lost forever.

Nevertheless Lycophron with the *Alexandra* has served his time-spirit well. The polished futility of the Alexandrian age, the dichotomy of literary minds that had severed their means of communication with the world at large, and the rootless uncertainty of a top-heavy commercial civilization, are brought to their full focus in his negative epic. Its efforts to break down the old cultural limitations of form and language are a sign of artistic self-doubt, of inner despair in which chaos and dissonance have stultified the creative impulse.

That involuted Alexandrian obscurity for its own sake, with the consequent divorce of the artist from the great majority of his contemporaries, is as characteristic of our age as of Lycophron's. Sharing the same time spirit, we respond to the atmosphere of *Ulysses* and *Finnegans Wake*—and our cultural void, the fears and frustrations of the uncertain modern world makes us sense our emotional kinship with Joyce's nihilistic achievement.

It is extremely doubtful, however, if the next generation or two—to look no further ahead—will either tolerate or comprehend the transcendent estimate of Joyce's work current in our time. Lycophron held meaning only for his immediate age. Less than a hundred years after his death he was condemned by Lucian, and in Augustan times he was looked on by the Roman literati as a wilfully complex poetaster. The two books of Joyce's maturity may well within a similar period of time seem as incomprehensible as the

Alexandra, and Joyce himself as ponderous as the now unreadable Klopstock who 200 years ago also seemed a mediator between heaven and earth.

The test of permanence in literature is truth and clarity. Those few masterpieces that stand out as immortal within the brief limits of human history, tower above their age with its adventitious circumstances of dress, customs, politics, language, and even civilization. The art form that has meaning only for its own generation is quickly submerged in the next. A relatively few basic factors endure through the diverse strata of existence—ambition, conflict, love, death and the mystery of time's passing.

Joyce maintained that he could do anything he wanted with language, forgetting in his logomathic isolation that language is at best a faulty tool, a poor substitute for life itself. His error was that of Lycophron and the Alexandrians. The world artist makes no such mistake. Sharing a common humanity, his genius makes it articulate, preserving in his own work those enduring qualities of our own unenduring lives to which men of all ages can give their inner response. When it lacks such qualities art becomes Hellenistic, developing such monstrous curiosities as the *Alexandra* or *Finnegans Wake*, that survive, when they do at all, like mastodons accidentally imbedded in time's glacier.

KAFKA

There have been few modern authors for whom such high claims have been made as Franz Kafka. The enigmatic quality of his writing has offered a variety of interpretations which though at times contradictory are none the less absolute. He has been held to be one of the handful of permanently significant artists of our era. By some critics his work is seen as a new justification of the ways of God to man, a striving with the Divine comparable to Job's. Others have found in Kafka the irreconcilable dualism of the finite and the infinite, still others the dilemma of modern man for whom God is dead and yet persists as an object of longing. A quite opposite school of interpretation sees in Kafka's novels the first literary embodiment of Freud's theories, a panorama of the states of consciousness according to the psychoanalytic movement. To a third group, Kafka in his autobiographical heroes exemplifies the loneliness and hermetic isolation of the individual in the modern world. More than any other writer, it is said, he has probed to the depths and hidden corners of the contemporary soul. Some indeed view Kafka as a seer whose telepathic awareness sensed in advance the emergence of Hitlerism and the rise of the slave states with their patterns of terror and persecution that tremble prophetically in his pages.

In our dark and tragic era when thought recoils on itself and the undefined and the obscure claim their pre-eminence over the rational and the precise, it is widely held that the only approach to the problem of existence is through the irrational. Each generation brings forth its own responses to the mysteries of life, death, and the irrevocable flow of time—if only in the negation of turning away. Kafka's bloodless world of unlogic has seemed prophetic to the present generation. Whatever his ultimate value, his sustained obscurity is a determinative of a period marked by the divorce of art from the common man, by the suspicion of popularity, and the cabalistic withdrawal of the intellectuals to their private cults.

During his lifetime Kafka was a minor figure on the outskirts of expressionism, known for little more than a few sketches and short stories. It was only after his death in 1924 and the subsequent publication by his friend and biographer Max Brod of the three novels, *America*, *The Trial* and *The Castle* that his reputation began to take hold. Brod through his almost fanatical efforts brought the Kafka vogue into being. By a process of intuition independent of evidence he was early convinced of his friend's greatness. In 1907, long before Kafka had published anything and when his total written work consisted of only a scattering of impressionistic vignettes, Brod in an article in the Berlin *Gegenwart* claimed him as one of the pre-eminent contemporary literary figures. Kafka himself when he was dying of tuberculosis asked that his manuscripts be destroyed at his death. But in spite of Kafka's wishes Brod could not bring himself to carry this out, and it was due to his insistence that his friend's works at last appeared in print. They appeared at the psychological moment. These hallucinatory novels struck a sympathetic response among the deracinated intellectuals of the Weimar Republic. The atmosphere of Germany then, under its patchwork veneer of democratic liberalism, was one of a shattered cosmos. Kafka in his morbid isolation became for many Germans a retreat from the broken world of reality to a private world of introspection. For others he offered, at least in Brod's interpretation, a kind of non-religious mystical escape, a solace for the intellectual's loss of nerve in a Europe that was no longer a civilization of fixed values but a 'waiting for the end'.

In the uneasy 'thirties the novels were translated into English, and the Kafka problem became a new source of exegesis for *avant-garde* thinking, a kind of literary snobbism that held up his incomprehensibility to the Philistines. After the war Kafka was canonized by the existentialists as a man of defiance who had dared to oppose his individual ego to the nihilistic universe. By the 'fifties he had become a fixture of the little reviews and reached the fringes of the suburban intelligentsia.

Even the most casual reading of Kafka gives the impression of unreality, of displacement, of a loss of contact with ordinary life as known to most men. Basically his writings are a dream-autobiography set in a pathological isolation that is symbolic of his own existence. 'I felt cut off from everything', he wrote in a fragmentary sketch of his childhood. He was always cut off. His life, except for the last few, ailing years, was spent in his native city of Prague, which for him as a German Jew was a double isolation. The lives of the Czech majority were foreign to him. He attended an authoritarian German secondary school, leaving his home each morning, returning each afternoon, a lonely brooding child dutifully following the familiar pattern of unfamiliar streets like a character in one of his own stories. The people he passed talked in strange syllables. Except for servants he never came in contact with them. He did not even have the consolation of being rooted in a homogeneous caste group, for within the Prague German enclave itself he belonged to the denationalized Jewish minority. Throughout Kafka's writings the unknown city of his fantasy is always Prague—by whatever name it may be called—although one can rarely identify it tangibly, for it is as unreal, as nebulous as the half-Gothic half-Baroque city with its babble of tongues must have been to the small boy on his way to the German Gymnasium in the Old Town Square. The environment that shaped Kafka was, as a Czech writer recently stated, the uniquely pathological situation of the Prague German-Jewish population. Both as a German and as a Jew Kafka was an outcast, a man apart, with roots neither in Imperial Germany nor in the Hebraic tradition.

Prague remained the form, but the substance of Kafka's isolated personality was developed in his family circle, a circle closed like a magic band, from which he was able to break away only towards the end of his life. His childhood fixed the pattern that psychoanalytic literature has since made familiar; the over-attachment to the mother, the ambivalent attitude to the father who dominates the domestic scene as an absolute ruler against whom it is both necessary and impossible to revolt. Kafka could never make up his mind whether he loved or hated his father, and his very doubt filled him with a constant sense of guilt. In his later years he once said that he wanted to group everything he had written under the collective title, *The Attempt To Escape From Father*.

The elder Kafka was a self-made merchant, aggressive, opinionated, essentially insignificant. Yet for his son he loomed up as a pentateuchal figure bearing the power of the commandments. Even in Kafka's maturity his father remained the focal point in his writings, the autocratic voice of authority that appeared protean-wise as the implacable Court in *The Trial*, the arbitrary officialdom of *The Castle*, the uncle (among others) in *America*, the father himself in *The Judgement*, the old Commandant of *In The Penal Colony*. Most of Kafka's life was a defence against his father, and it is this struggle re-enacted in different forms that is the one enduring factor throughout his work. Never was he able to reach emotional maturity. At the age of thirty-six, five years before his death, he was still grappling with the problem of his father, still trying to clarify their mutual relationship. It was then that he wrote his *Letter To My Father*, an almost book-length apologia which his mother wisely prevented the father from seeing. 'I believe', he concluded, 'it (the letter) comes so close to truth that it should bring a little peace to both of us, and make living and dying somewhat easier.'

In the *Letter* he reconstructed his life as a series of efforts to break away from the egocentric father whom he both feared and admired and whom he himself would have liked to be beyond anyone else. 'You', he wrote, 'are a real Kafka in strength, health, appetite, vocal power, speaking ability, self-approval, sophistication, perseverance, presence of mind, knowledge of people, and in a certain magnanimity. Of course with

49

all the advantages are combined their corresponding weaknesses and faults, into which you are plunged by your disposition and, at times, by your temper.'

The letter is a strange mixture of reproaches to his father, reproaches to himself and a longing for reconciliation with the man whose approval he wanted far more than any literary success and which he was never to attain.

Kafka lived as a solitary child in an alien city. His two older brothers died in childhood and his first sister was born only after he was six, too late to give him any sense of companionship. Left for the most part in the care of governesses while both parents worked, he early lost the innate volatility common to most children. In his diary he speaks of being afraid then of mirrors because they showed his inescapable ugliness. Unsatisfactory as his home was, his need for warmth and reassurance, and his longing for an unrealizable close-knit family life threw him back on it, the very strength of his attachment being a blind effort to convince himself against the evidence that it was an organic unity in which he shared. All the concomitant facts of his life, his over-attachment to his mother, his fearful admiration for his father, his inability for forty years to break away from his surroundings, stemmed from that early psychic malaise, that imbalance of his childhood against which he did not have the strength to revolt. 'Where I lived', he explained in the letter to his father, 'I was repudiated, judged, suppressed, and although I tried my utmost to escape elsewhere, it never could amount to anything, because it involved the impossible, something that was, with small exceptions, unattainable for my powers. . . .'

In the conflicting atmosphere of his home he developed with adolescence a mental sterility, a paralysis of the will that became integral to him. Home offered him, if not happiness, at least a retreat from the ominous and perplexing outer world which, as he reached maturity, he could less and less bring himself to face. From his university days he wanted to be a writer, but he never developed sufficient strength of will to strike out for himself and make a career of his chosen profession as did his friend Franz Werfel.

After finishing school he went on to the German University of Prague, where he decided to study law, not from any interest that he felt in it, but because, as he said, it seemed to him that the law was an indifferent profession which he could follow without injury to his ego. The study of jurisprudence he described as 'feeding mentally on sawdust'. Although before the first war it was customary among German and Austrian students to spend at least a year wandering from city to city and attending various universities for a semester or two before settling down to the specialized work of their doctorate, Kafka who might easily have passed a few semesters in Vienna or Munich or Berlin, stayed all his five university years in Prague.

On receiving his doctor's degree he remained the customary year attached without salary to a law court. Then with the same indifference that characterized his choice of studies he accepted the first position offered him, a minor post in an Italian insurance company. Later he managed to secure a place in the semi-governmental Workmen's Accident Insurance Institute for the Kingdom of Bohemia.

It was a position that Kafka filled conscientiously.

Yet, though the hours of eight to two were extra-ordinarily brief for those days, the business world was a galling burden to him. He felt his creative impulses thwarted both by the bureaucracy and by the demands made on him by his parents. He was a writer, without being able to write. His emotionally self-consuming existence was blocked of any outlet. Nevertheless he made no real attempt to change. Although Berlin was a vague promised land to him, he never seriously tried to arrange his life or his profession so that he could go there. Even in later years after what he called his 'break-through', when he was working on his novels and had rented one room in the old quarter of Prague where he studied and another where he slept, he still made a daily visit to his home and took most of his meals there.

At the age of thirty Kafka as a self-ordained writer with no other interest in life but that of literature had written nothing more than a few scraps and tag-ends. Two extracts from a phantasmagoric forty-page story of his were printed in the magazine *Hyperion* in 1909. The same year another piece, *The Aeroplanes At Brescia*, appeared, a competent journalistic account of a flying exhibition he had attended in Italy, written care-fully with an observant eye and a quiet humour. Finally there were the tenuous little sketches—some only a sentence long—that he later combined in his first book, *Contemplation*. They were impressionistic studies with expressionistic overtones, brief glimpses of isolated scenes, occasionally fantastic, but devoid of any basic significance.

Kafka's allegorical short story, *The Metamorphosis*, gives a singularly revealing picture of the author in relation to his family at this period. It is a remarkable *tour de force*, awkward in dialogue as are all his works, yet, after the initial fable is accepted, one of the most straightforward and effective pieces he wrote. In brief it is the author's private opinion of himself, for the protagonist, Gregor Samsa the Prague commercial traveller, is even to his name only a thinly veiled auto-biographical figure.

Gregor is a minor agent of a large company, in a job that he would have quitted long ago except that he is under the necessity of supporting his parents and his younger sister. One rainy morning he suddenly wakes up to find himself transformed into a giant millipede with a brown chitin-encased body. The rest of the story deals with Gregor's transformation in its effect on his family, and their attitude towards him in his excruciating situation.

After their first appalling encounter with him as an insect, in which significantly his father picks up a stick and drives his vermin son back into his bedroom, they keep him locked up there, concealed as an unspeakably shameful secret that gradually undermines their family existence. Gregor's sister at first feeds him out of pity, but later neglects him. Only his mother in spite of her horror at this noxious bug never forgets that it is still her unfortunate son. Once when Gregor had wandered out of his bedroom and created a panic in the household, his father in a rage would have beaten him to death but for his mother's pathetic intercession. Finally the tenderness and love that in, spite of his terrible outer change, he has still kept for his family make him realize that his only way to aid them is to die. In any case he has by the end of the year become indifferent to life. The morning following his awareness of this, the charwoman finds his corpse on the floor, and being a matter-of-fact woman, first calls the parents and then disposes of the body in her own way. This day of Gregor's death is a liberation for his suffering family which they celebrate by making an excursion into the country, free at last of the dreadful shadow of their son.

In *The Metamorphosis* Kafka has reversed his dependence on his family to making them depend on him, but otherwise it is a self-portrait. All the morbid lacerating qualities of his mind, his guilt consciousness, his self-hate, are dramatized in the crawling insect, the creature that longs for normality, for the unity and love of family life, and to whom such things are forever barred.

Until his thirtieth year Kafka had considered himself a predetermined bachelor. At that time, however, he met Felice Bauer, the F.B. of his diaries, a strong-minded young woman with whom he immediately fell in love and to whom he later became engaged. It was an engagement that lasted with distressing vacillations on his part for five years. Although he was devoted to Felice, he could never bring himself to take the final decisive step of marriage. He still felt bound to his family; his tentative efforts to liberate himself were never vigorous and never wholly sincere. Eventually F.B. had to give him up. Marriage was for a long time the subject of much inconclusive thought on his part. His often-mentioned interest in Kierkegaard first developed, not from any mystical affinity, but from the latter's discussion of marriage in *Either/Or*.

Even though he was never to marry F.B., his

emotional and physical relationship with her did succeed in giving him an artistic release, his 'break-through' as he called it. A short while after their meeting he suddenly discovered that the barriers that had hindered him from writing had broken down. One evening he sat all night in a trance-like state composing his short story, *The Judgement*. It was the first work of his adult writing period. Subsequently he often composed in this manner.

The Judgement, like the three novels, is a recollection of a dream, with all the illogic and arbitrary action of the dream-state. The year after Kafka had finished it, when he was engaged on *The Metamorphosis* and *America*, he wrote in his diary: 'What my fate will be as a writer is very simple. My talent for portraying my dream-like inner life has thrust all other matters into the background; my life has dwindled dreadfully, nor will it cease to dwindle.'

As a story *The Judgement* is an unrelated sequence of events that allow themselves, like the novels, to be interpreted in several ways according to the bent of the interpreter. The one clear central theme, however, is that of the father-son conflict. At the beginning of *The Judgement* Georg Bendemann, a young merchant, is sitting in his room on a Sunday morning, having just finished a letter to an un-named friend of his in Russia telling him among other things of his engagement to a Frieda Brandenfeld. For some time he has hesitated to tell his friend either of this or of his recent business successes because of the latter's lack of success. Finally, after putting the letter in his pocket, he goes across a small lobby to his father's room. The aspect of the room is vague, the figure of the father in his fluttering dressing gown one of a giant. They talk of the friend in Russia and Georg mentions writing about his engagement, whereupon the father suddenly expresses doubt that the friend in Russia exists. Instead of becoming angry or trying to argue, Georg becomes embarrassed and says that a thousand friends would not make up for his father. As if the latter were ailing —although this has not been previously indicated— Georg now leads him back to his own room and tries to persuade him to lie down there.

The old man insists again that there is no friend in Russia. Georg reminds him of the times the friend had visited them in the past, meanwhile carrying his father in his arms to the bed, where he covers him with a blanket. Then in a nightmare sequence the old man springs up until he touches the ceiling, shouting that he knew the friend after all, that this friend would have been a son after his own heart, and that his son has been playing him false all these years. He then accuses his son of disgracing his mother's memory, betraying his friend and putting his father to bed in order to make free with F., and he tells Georg that he, the father, has been representing the friend all these years. After a crescendo of accusations the father finally exclaims, 'I sentence you to death by drowning!' Georg, hearing these words, dashes down the flight of steps, out across the roadway and towards the river, swinging himself over the bridge rails and finally letting himself drop into the water. Just as he drops, however, he calls out in a low voice, 'Dear parents, I have always loved you.'

Beneath the incoherent surface of *The Judgement* the ramifications of Kafka's family relationship and his new relationship to his fiancée are so apparent that it seems Kafka himself should have been instantly aware of their symbolic significance. Yet, strangely enough, he was not, for according to his diary the autobiographical basis of the story came later as a complete surprise to him. 'Georg', he writes, as if he were making a discovery, 'has the same number of letters as Franz. In Bendemann the "mann" is there only to strengthen the syllable "Bende" [bonds] in case of any unseen possibilities in the story. But Bende has the same number of letters as Kafka and the vowel "e" is repeated in the same position as the vowel "a" in Kafka.

'Frieda has exactly the same number of letters as F, and begins with the same letter; Brandenfeld begins with the same letter as B.'

One may if one wishes find cosmic overtones in the paucity of *The Judgement* and see in this father-son struggle a strife between two worlds. One may see the father as God the Father, and Georg as mankind. Or equally if one wishes one may view Georg's fate as that of the Weimar Republic and the father as the Reich. A Freudian interpretation would produce other results, as would a Marxian.

It is the inherent vagueness of Kafka, the *non-sequitur* design persisting through his works that has offered such an unrivalled field for commentators and critics. The intricate jargon of the new secular scholasticism has created the Kafka problem. Within his unresolved pages great truths are supposed to lie hidden, perhaps even the ultimate revelation of our age.

Kafka's writings were formed by German expressionism and bear its stamp throughout. His actual style, however, as opposed to his subject-matter is a clear, almost technical German, classical in the arid eighteenth-century sense, segregated from the common tongue. Kafka's language was an artificial literary creation. He knew no Germans beyond his own limited circle. There was no way that he, shut off in the Prague Ghetto, could come in contact with colloquial speech.

His expressionism was a further restricting barrier. Expressionism, with its elimination of what is considered superfluous details to get at the thing-in-itself, produced only a colourless world of form and motion. Kafka's novels are made up of interiors that dissolve as we look at them, of long vistas of streets where the sun never shines, the wind never blows. There is an absence of the breath of life; there are no human beings, but rather pale phantoms that appear from nowhere and fade away. Kafka's flat two-dimensional landscape resembles an early moving picture, progressing jerkily with exaggerated gestures and flickering effects of light and shadow.

America, the first of his novels, follows the adventures of a sixteen-year-old German, Karl Rossman, in the United States, a United States that is like some kind of lunar landscape with fitful recollections of Europe. Again there is the same similarity in name between Karl Rossman and Franz Kafka as well as the same twisted thread of father-son relationship, for Karl has been deported by his family. The opening chapter with its approach to New York Harbour—an elaboration of a dream mentioned in Kafka's diary—is like the action of the rest of the book. If seen from a realistic point of view it becomes a series of incomprehensibly disconnected events. That such events are not decipherable on a rational plane seems self-evident. The tradition of naturalism having long since exhausted itself with Zola, clarity is not, according to Kafka apologists, a demand that the reader should in any way make. Rather the actions of Karl Rossmann, of Joseph K. in *The Trial* and of K. in *The Castle* are symbols that Kafka in his subliminal world has succeeded in implanting with general validity. For the apologists Kafka has written the *Pilgrim's Progress* of an age of disbelief.

In Kafka's trilogy, just as in *The Judgement*, one can find the explanation of one's choice. According to the psychoanalytic explanation Karl Rossmann's journey with its various adventures is a striving to attain heterosexual stability. To a more mystically-minded critic 'Karl's path of suffering ends, like the Book of Job, in contact with God who confirms to man that he has "accepted" him in this inexplicable world, and has not forgotten him.'[1]

Charles Neider in *The Frozen Sea* makes detailed analyses of *The Trial* and *The Castle*, following an orthodox Freudian interpretation. It is an impressive feat. The author has left no stone unturned, missed no post or pot-hole, dwelling or common utensil, endowing them all even to the telephone with their special sexual significance. He overlooks no overt gesture. There may be some substance to his claim that Kafka once underwent partial analysis. Whether or not he is justified in claiming that *The Trial* and *The Castle* are contour maps of the mind deliberately supplied by Kafka with Freudian conventional signs to indicate each route, is another matter. From what Kafka said

[1] Herbert Tauber, *Franz Kafka* (Secker & Warburg, 1948), p. 54.

himself he seems to have composed without any effort at direct control. In his diary he mentions writing *The Giant Mole* 'almost without knowing it', and of another story, a prelude to *The Trial*, he found the significance did not dawn on him until he read it aloud to F.B.

Kafka's novels are the uneasy dreaming of a troubled mind. Karl Rossmann stays in New York in houses as grotesque as half-completed Hollywood sets, he starts from there on his travels against a stage background where larks fly up in the alien air and the vague grim buildings recall only the drabness of central European suburbs. There is no continuity, no plot, no obvious reason when Karl leaves the road and the scene shifts to a hotel. At first the hotel seems a kind of country inn, then it becomes a Metropole with thirty lifts and 5,000 guests. Because there are no points of reference, because the situations never convince, the tedium of these pages becomes overwhelming. After more inexplicable occurrences in a dingy block of flats one follows Rossmann to the Nature Theatre of Oklahoma, where, before a race course that is being used as a recruiting centre for the theatre cast, 'hundreds of women dressed as angels in white robes with great wings on their shoulders were blowing on long trumpets that glittered like gold.' They stand on columns, and every two hours they are relieved by a group of men dressed as devils, half of whom blow trumpets, the rest beating on drums. The incident is variously considered to be a satire on the Church and a promise of salvation. It is with Rossmann's entrance into this papier mâché heaven that the book ends.

In *The Trial* there is at least the consistent quality of

persecution. Joseph K. (Kafka) is arrested, judged, condemned and executed by a nebulous Court of vague authority acting in as arbitrary a manner as did the father of *The Judgement*. He does not know why, and in the end he does not protest. One is reminded of the trial in *Alice in Wonderland* and the Queen's 'Sentence first—verdict afterward!', for in Kafka's Court, as is later explained, an acquittal is usually followed by a re-arrest, then possibly by another acquittal and another arrest in ending sequence.

Joseph K. is bank employee living in a boarding house who wakes one morning to find himself arrested for no ostensible reason by two strangely-dressed warders. He is ordered to dress and is conducted to an inspector installed in the next room, and after a short baffling interview is told that he may carry on with his daily work at the bank as usual. Some time afterwards he is informed by telephone that an inquiry into his case will take place the following Sunday.

The inquiry is held on the fifth floor of a slum tenement as oppressively weird as the one in *America*. From there the logic of events breaks down, among strange advocates, in and out of courts that are like kangaroo courts, inside the parody of a cathedral, with sudden shifts of scene and spectral characters that come and go. According to Neider, *The Trial* presents a detailed account of the dynamics of the castration complex.[1] John Kelly in his essay, included in *The Kafka Problem*, would have it an 'allegory of man's relations with God in terms of a Calvinistic theology'.[2]

[1] *The Frozen Sea* (Oxford, 1948). See page 172. 'The warders, like K's assistants in *The Castle*, symbolize Joseph K.'s testicles and his deficient sexuality.'

[2] *New Directions*, 1946, p. 151.

Again, there are no valid reference points. Joseph K's advocate whom he seeks out in a run-down flat, is a senile bedridden old man. The Court itself is peopled by shabby venal officials, unpredictable and capricious, ignorant of jurisprudence, readers of pornographic books. It may be said, just as with the arbitrary officials of *The Castle*, that the Court represents the higher authority of God, a state incomprehensible to man and so not to be judged by his values. There is a parallel case in *The Castle* where a young woman receives an obscene letter from one of the officials of the inaccessible Castle—claimed by Brod and others to represent the Divine Grace—and because she refuses to answer it brings ruin on her family. According to the theological interpretation her error was in judging the Divine by her own mundane standards.

The consistent quality of *The Castle* is in the opposition and contrast between the mysterious castle on its hill and the village below it to which K., a land surveyor appointed by the Castle, arrives. He never reaches the goal of the Castle nor on the other hand in his stay in the anonymous village does he ever find himself accepted into the community. During his time there he flounders in a web of circumstances similar to Joseph K.'s, there are much the same *non-sequiturs*, the same two-dimensional landscape, the same interminable stylized conversations. The only place that Kafka seems to shed his fantasy and bring his narrative to life is in the seduction scene with the barmaid Frieda in the inn. It is a recurring theme with Kafka, that one finds vividly recollected in the first chapter of *America*, and again in the brief encounter with the advocate's servant Leni in *The Trial*. As Eisner explained, the frequent appearance of Czech serving women in Kafka's work was a characteristic of German Prague. Kafka in all probability received his sexual initiation from some such woman, and the naturalistic recollection of it persists in breaking through his trance-like pages.

Edwin Muir, Kafka's English translator, found the subject-matter of both *The Trial* and *The Castle* as 'human life wherever it is touched by the powers which all religions have acknowledged, by divine law and divine grace'.[1] To Neider *The Castle* is 'the tale of the quest for the unconscious by some one who has reached the preconscious. The village is the preconscious and the castle the unconscious.'[2] Kafka himself in the letter to his father wrote: 'My writings are about you. I merely poured into them what I could not pour out on your breast. They were a deliberately prolonged fare-well, imposed by you, certainly, but given a direction determined by myself.' Read in the light of Kafka's admission it is clear that the one motivating force of both *The Trial* and *The Castle* is the father conflict, and the forbidding castle as the emblem of authority becomes the unapproachable father figure.

There are other direct autobiographical traces— Kafka, for example, began the original draft of *The Castle* in the first person. Both Joseph K. and K. are isolated bachelors. The loneliness of those dim streets and interiors is the loneliness of Prague. But the father is the dominant motif. Understanding this, one is impelled to ask just what is the larger validity of this neurotic striving.

Kafka, sick in mind and body, took the murky

[1] Introduction to *The Castle* (Secker & Warburg), pp. vi-vii.
[2] op. cit., p. 129.

images that welled up inside him and spun them out in a spectral realm. His novels are fragments. There is no logic that requires them ever to come to an end. In his pages the phantoms of expressionism move through a dream world, not the magic world of Xanadu, but the apathetic dreariness of the Prague enclave. Kafka's primary significance is not in his work, which lacks those permanent values by which works of art survive, but in the extraordinary valuation set on him. He has provided almost inexhaustible material for the sciolists and mystagogues of our era. More clearly than any other literary figure of these times he demonstrates the retreat from meaning, the flight of the intellectual into a Babel tower of symbols, the snob rejection of communicability that reaches the last stages of the absurd in surrealism.

Art is a subliminal impulse refined by conscious judgement. When, however, consciousness is suspended the effect is monstrous. Blake's prophetic books are monstrous, yet in spite of their tortuous symbolism often touched with pure poetry. Kafka is monstrous without being a poet. One senses his guilt, his feelings of persecution, his loneliness, but they are gross ore. His self-consuming art lacks substance. It can become a problem for scholiasts but it will not move ordinary men.

In the last year of his life Kafka did finally break away from his family, going to live in Berlin with a young Polish Jewess whom he had met casually at a summer resort. But by then he was mortally ill with tuberculosis. However, for a time at least he achieved a belated happiness. His fragmentary writings of this period are a congealed expressionism, with the authoritarian father figure at last banished. It may be, as in his sketch *A Fasting Showman*, that Kafka saw himself as an artist who had created only for himself out of his inner need, and consequently when he attained a delayed objectivity he had no further use for his subjective novels. In any case, facing death, regretting the fleeting quality of his happiness, he wished the manuscripts destroyed. As for his much-discussed religious beliefs, his aphorisms and meditations are ambiguous witnesses. He did not follow a formal religion, he was sadly aware of the infinite gap between man and the universe, he made an occasional reference to reincarnation, but there is no real evidence of his faith in a transcendant God. When he spoke of dying as 'surrendering a nothing to a nothing' it was probably his final belief.

One of the most lucid definitions of Kafka's art is found indirectly expressed in a sentence from his *Meditations*. 'Round about us', he wrote, 'the confusion of the senses, or the utmost receptivity of the senses, shows us only monsters and a kaleidoscopic play of images which is delightful or tiring according to the mood or the bruised condition of the individual.' It is a sick concept, but his withdrawn sickness is common to the intellectual climate of our age.

GERTRUDE STEIN

THE final significance of Gertrude Stein lies, not in her work, but in the fact that she was the first writer in English to express fully the disintegrative tendencies that have been the hall-mark of advanced western art movements from the latter part of the nineteenth century. Whether or not her writings in themselves have any permanent or even transient value they are nevertheless representative of the intellectual history of the times, and to that extent she was justified in calling herself the first twentieth-century author.

In the decade before 1914 when to the great majority of the people the established order seemed comfortably assured, there was a gathering mood of revolt among the younger generation of intellectuals that was one of the uneasy signs of the enveloping political crises to come. To the artist of the early century, sensitive to the time-spirit, the ultimate function of art was to create a new super-reality through the destruction of traditional forms. Ordinary words and syntax had become outworn instruments too primitive to reveal the indefinable cosmic essence that flickered like a will o' the wisp in the depths of the mind. Language was to be reformed, remoulded, that through its revealed possibilities it might approach the ultimate secret of man's being. The new forms had to be hammered out on the anvil of the unconscious. Old languages, old words in their old order, had become stale and trivial. There was nothing more to be said in the conventional sense of the word. Eugene Jolas in a *Transition* manifesto of the 'thirties calling for a revolution in language, asserted that in his career he had already exhausted the possibilities of three European tongues.

A recent evaluation of Gertrude Stein maintains that 'it is perfectly possible that the first half of this century, in which everything has been wildly disconnected and at the same time almost everything is made to connect with anything else, may find its most exact meaning in the word "steinesque." '[1]

Such a point of view is no longer as common today as it was, although there is still a loyal clique that feels, as did Virgil Thomson, that Gertrude Stein has become 'a founding Father of her century as her reward for having long ago, and completely, dominaated her language'. She, the innovator, the original expatriate, has become somewhat eclipsed by her more spectacular successors, writers of greater fire and depth. The wider appeal that she created for herself in later life with the publication of *The Autobiography of Alice B. Toklas*, a book that approached best seller popularity, alienated the *avant-garde* circle of which she had been one of the pundits. In her last days she developed into a curiosity, an imposing figure that for literary-minded Americans became one of the sights of Paris.

Except for one circumstance her life contains little of personal significance beyond the generally known features. It was a life of studied uneventfulness, one on which the external world with its wars, depressions

[1] Donald Sutherland, *Gertrude Stein: A Biography of Her Work* (Yale University Press, 1951), p. 85.

and social overturns had only a superficial effect. She was born in 1874 in Baltimore of German-Jewish parents and brought up in California as one of a large family. When she was eighteen she came east to the recently-established Radcliffe College, a female annex of Harvard. She appeared then a typical blue-stocking, the new woman of the late 'nineties. Her Radcliffe English themes show no more than the determined cleverness of an average intellectual young woman almost pugnaciously conscious of her emancipation. She studied under William James and later claimed that he had considered her his most brilliant woman student, an assertion her brother Leo later denied. In any case it was as a student of James that she first became aware of the form and structure of language and some of its psychological implications. During this undergraduate period she collaborated in certain experiments in automatic writing, the results of which were published in *The Psychological Review*.[1]

Later she came to regret the publication of this article, giving substance as it did to the claim that the disaggregation of her later experimental work was a result of writing uncontrolled by the conscious centres of the mind—an accusation that by its partial truth brought testy denials from her years afterwards both in her autobiographies and in her lectures.

She herself admitted that the method of writing afterward to be developed in *Three Lives* and *The Making of Americans* already showed itself in the *Psychological Review* article, but she quite rightly denied that

[1] Leon M. Solomons and Gertrude Stein, *Normal Motor Automatism* (*The Psychological Review*, Vol. III, No. 5, September 1896).

this method could be considered automatic.[1] Her work lacks the prerequisite of true automatic writing, the integrating of a second personality, the creation of a unique cosmology such as one finds in Blake's prophetic books, or even the projection of a dream-world like the Brontës' *Gondal*. Whatever her creative method, the impulse behind it was self-conscious.

After graduating from Radcliffe she spent several years studying medicine at Johns Hopkins, years that seem to have had no marked influence on her life. She took no degree. Most of her summers were spent in Europe. Whether or not she was the dilettante student that her brother Leo later made out, her medical studies were inconsequential in her later development. Leo Stein had been living in Florence for several years when Gertrude, after leaving Johns Hopkins, joined him there. They spent the winter in London, then she returned to New York and he went on to France. The next year, 1903, she left America for good, following her brother to Paris, where she made her home with him in the little house at 27 rue de Fleurus that was to become so well-known to the generation of expatriates. On her arrival she began to write her premature novel, *Things As They Are*, a book that she in later years maintained that she had completely forgotten.

There seems to have been no overpowering reason

[1] See Ronald B. Levinson's article in *The American Psychological Review*, Vol. LIV, No. 1, January 1941, p. 128. 'It is difficult not to suppose at least an initial arousal and some permanent direction of interest toward the philosophy of grammar, as having passed from the persuasive teacher (James) to the girl whom he evaluated as the most brilliant of all his female students. . . . It is this intellectual concern with linguistic experimentation, though one may quite deny the success of the experiments, which may supply a clue for distinguishing the products of Miss Stein's literary workshop from those earlier automatic fruits of the Harvard Laboratory of Psychology.'

for Gertrude Stein's quitting the United States when she did—unless it can be found in the pages of *Things As They Are*—nothing of the emotional urgency that sent Henry James and T. S. Eliot across the Atlantic. She was not conscious of any alienation from America, never regarded herself dramatically as an exile as did James Joyce. All her life she remained insistently American with an uncritical patriotism deriving from her elementary school memories. She did not seem even to be searching for personal freedom, but lived contentedly under the shadow of her brother.

In those days she was obscured by Leo's knowledge of art and aesthetics, his assured if pedantic manner of exposition. Leo Stein was, as Hutchins Hapgood then saw him, 'the great spirit of twenty-seven rue de Fleurus'. His was the original interest in Cézanne. He was the first of his contemporaries to take up Matisse and Picasso and buy their pictures when their names meant nothing. In that studio adjoining the rue de Fleurus house, hung with pictures then shocking to the eye, he explained and elucidated his theories of art to an expanding group of friends and acquaintances while his sister sat quietly in the background and listened with the rest. Sometimes, according to Mabel Dodge, she had a puzzled look to her eyes as the conversation skirted her.

Things As They Are, written when Gertrude Stein was in her thirtieth year, is an account of a triangular love affair between three young American women, one of whom is obviously the author. Such a book, possibly the first study of female inversion in English, could not be considered publishable at the time, and there is no evidence that Gertrude Stein made any effort to have it printed.

It is a book written under the compulsive influence of an emotional crisis, and the author in groping to express herself is not concerned with the problem of style. *Things As They Are* has the hothouse atmosphere that one finds in *The Well of Loneliness*, the trembling on the edge of hysteria without adequate motivation, a veiled allusiveness that makes one uncertain whether the author is describing mental or physical states. Only a few times is the veil dropped and the flesh laid bare.

On the whole the effect of *Things As They Are* is flat, yet nevertheless for all its flatness this small book is the most directly felt piece that Gertrude Stein ever wrote. From this point it was as if she turned her back on herself, deliberately thrust her feelings behind her and chose to develop her writing not as an emotional re-creation of past experience but as a form of experimentation akin to the post-impressionistic tendencies in painting with which, thanks to her brother, she was coming in contact. Between *Things As They Are*, written in 1903, and *The Autobiography of Alice B. Toklas*, written thirty years later, the body of her work is characterized by a deliberate and extraordinary absence of feeling.

Once she had resolved the personal conflict that lay behind her early novelette, she fixed herself on a writing career, uncertain of subject matter and now lacking inspiration, but with a compulsive desire for fame and an unshakeable conviction that she could attain it. As she admitted later, she wanted to be a lion, and the only way that seemed possible to her was by her pen. During this period she formed the close association with Miss Toklas that was to last the rest of her days and confirm the dichotomy between her private life and her work. In *Things As They Are* she had cried out against an intolerable hurt. It was her first and last attempt to reveal her inner self, for even her later autobiographies in their artful artlessness fail to show any significant underlying emotion. Miss Toklas, the most important person in Gertrude Stein's life, is in spite of the title of the first autobiographic volume an undefined and unaccountable figure. Gertrude Stein found her refuge in a retrogressive technique. With *The Making of Americans* she was to pass into a stage of cold aloofness where it is impossible to determine her feelings, her cultural background or her point of view.

She approached her next book with a firm determination to achieve greatness. But after *Things As They Are* she had shut off the direct sources of her inspiration, and until she fixed on style, until she went back, not to her feelings, but to the linguistic experiment she had made a decade earlier in the Harvard Laboratory, her approach was uncertain. *Three Lives* is her transitional piece.

These three stories contain echoes of her student days in Baltimore, although in no case do they involve her personally. For the most part they derive from the servant girls she employed at this time or—as in the central story, *Melanctha*—from the brief excursions she made into the slums during her period of obstetrical training. She had just been translating Flaubert's *Un Coeur Simple* and, as she herself admitted, it was under its influence that she began her first story, *The Good Anna*. Anna, like Flaubert's Félicité, is a faithful servant who serves her family with a single and simple-minded devotion. In the end like Félicité she dies. Flaubert's outline is followed without much variation, but there the parallel ceases. Instead of his supple meticulously-contrived prose, Gertrude Stein has evolved a top-heavy style with the beginnings of that puerile repetitiveness that she was to develop further in *Melanctha* and carry to such ponderous lengths in *The Making of Americans*.

The Gentle Lena, placed last in the book but written second, is the story of a dull-witted German servant girl who marries and also finally dies. Both pattern and method resemble *The Good Anna*, although the style itself tends to become more redundant.

Only in the story, *Melanctha*, does Gertrude Stein establish her characteristic mode of expression. As she herself later wrote, *Melanctha* is the beginning of her revolutionary work, and if looked at from the point of view of language distortion her remark that it was the first definite step away from the nineteenth and into the twentieth century in literature is also true, for it is one of the source documents of the twentieth-century reaction against form and meaning.

Melanctha is the account of a headstrong mulatto girl who rejects one lover, is rejected in turn by another, and without apparent motivation dies at the end of the story. It has been claimed as the first mature treatment of the Negro in American literature, although in actual fact Gertrude Stein knew nothing about Negroes. Even at the turn of the century it is not possible to imagine a young coloured doctor, a medical school graduate, talking in the character of her Jeff Campbell: 'Poor Melanctha, she don't know any way to be real honest, but no matter, I sure do love her and I be good if only she will let me.' Such a contrived lingo bears no resemblance even to uneducated Negro speech. But in fact *Melanctha* was not planned originally as a Negro story. That part of it came to Gertrude Stein as an afterthought, and the result is a burnt-cork lack of authenticity. As she stated in her autobiography, the incidents that she wove into *Melanctha* were often those she noted on her walks in Montmartre.

Melanctha, much longer than the other two, is much less a story. As the emphasis turns to technique, the outline and the action blur under the iteration of the piled-up phrases. 'It is very hard for Jeff Campbell to make all this way of doing, right, inside him. If Jeff Campbell could not be straight out, and real honest, he could never be very strong inside him. Now Melanctha, with her making him feel, always, how good she was and how very much she suffered in him, made him always go so fast then, he could not be strong then, to feel things out straight then inside him. Always now when he was with her, he was being more, than he could already yet, be feeling for her. Always now, with her, he had something inside him always holding in him, always now, with her, he was far ahead of his own feelings.' Here the style of *The Making of Americans* becomes apparent, if not as yet fixed, the elephantine prose, the trip-hammer weight of repetition.

In the *Psychological Review* article the authors' explanation of what they called 'spontaneous automatic writing' is not so much an explanation as a foreshadowing of the body of Gertrude Stein's later work. 'This (the automatic writing)', they declared, 'became quite easy after a little practice. . . . Miss Stein found it sufficient distraction often to simply read what her arm wrote, but following three or four words behind her pencil. . . . Two very interesting phenomena were observed here for the first time.

'A MARKED TENDENCY TO REPETITION.—A phrase would seem to get into the head and keep repeating itself at every opportunity, and hang over from day to day even. The stuff written was grammatical, and the words and phrases fitted together all right, but there was not much connected thought. The unconscious was broken into every six or seven words by flashes of consciousness, so that one cannot be sure but what the slight element of connected thought which occasionally appeared was due to these flashes of consciousness. But the ability to write stuff that sounds all right, without consciousness, was fairly well demonstrated by the experiments. Here are a few specimens:

' "Hence there is no possible way of avoiding what I have spoken of, and if this is not believed by the people of whom you have spoken, then it is not possible to prevent the people of whom you have spoken so glibly. . . ."

'Here is a bit more poetical than intelligible: "When he could not be the longest and thus to be, and thus to be, the strongest."

'And here is one that is neither: "This long time when he did this best time, and he could thus have been bound, and in this long time, when he could be this to first use of this long time. . . ." '[1]

Any one of these specimens might have been taken from *The Making of Americans*.

[1] op. cit., pp. 505-6.

The following passage chosen from a later work demonstrates the same pattern, the phrase repeating itself, the grammatical 'stuff' that fits together without much connected thought. 'He says that he means that he will hear what he will hear when he can hear what he has heard and when he does hear what he has heard. He says that he knows what he says when he does say that he has said what he can say when he will say what he does say and he says that he means that he does know what he does hear when he hears what he has heard and he knows what he will hear and he says what he does say.'[1]

Having rejected her emotions as literary source material, and being deficient in inventiveness, Gertrude Stein, beginning with *Melanctha* and expanding to the word-mass of *The Making of Americans*, evolved her particular consciously unconscious method of writing. Although automatically conceived it was still subordinate to her conscious mind, a species of controlled spontaneity. She wrote *The Making of Americans* from carefully elaborated notes. Subsequently in *Tender Buttons* she described household objects directly in front of her. In both cases her method was the same. With pen in hand she would concentrate on the immediate fact facing her, whether note or object, letting the impulse take its free course from the given stimulus and writing down whatever thoughts occurred to her without making any effort to control or subjugate them. What she wrote she left unchanged. It was not automatic writing—for at the moment of composition she was aware of what her pen was producing—

[1] *Two: Gertrude Stein and Her Brother*, Vol. I of the Yale edition of the unpublished writings of Gertrude Stein (Yale University Press, 1951), p. 91.

but a kind of literary contemplation foreshadowed in the Harvard experiments when she had written: 'A trained subject can watch his automatic movements without interfering with their complete non-voluntariness.'

It was usually not until late in the evening that she began to write, and then she kept at it until morning and the noises of the street would bring her back to herself and send her off to bed. Her friend Mabel Dodge at the Villa Curonia wrote about her manner of work: 'Gertrude always worked at night. After everyone was asleep she used to sit at Edwin's table next door writing automatically in a long weak handwriting—four or five lines to the page—letting it ooze up from deep down inside her, down onto the paper with the least possible physical effort; she would cover a few pages so and leave them there and go to bed, and in the morning Alice would gather them up first thing and take them off and type them. Then she and Gertrude would always be so surprised and delighted at what she had written, for it had been done so unconsciously she'd have no idea what she'd said the night before!'[1]

Gertrude Stein considered *The Making of Americans* her highest achievement, as she herself proclaimed, 'the monumental work which was the beginning, really the beginning of modern writing.' With the monolithic self-assurance integral to her and which she developed increasingly through the years she ranked it with *A la Recherche du Temps Perdu* and *Ulysses* as the most important work of the century.

The Making of Americans in its original edition of

[1] *European Experiences* (Harcourt, Brace & Co.), p. 328.

half a million words is one of the longest novels in English. Written over a five-year period from 1906 to 1911, it was first privately printed in 1925. In 1934 a trade edition, reduced to about a quarter of the original novel, appeared in the United States.

In outline it is the history of the author's family. She explained it later in her autobiography: 'In *The Making of Americans* I wrote about our family. I made it like a novel and I took a piece of one person and mixed it with a piece of another one and then I found that it was not interesting and instead I described everything. I had the idea of describing every one, every one who could or would or had been living, but in the beginning I did give a real description of how our family lived in East Oakland, and how everything looked as I had seen it then.'

From the notes and charts of her various relatives and friends that Gertrude Stein prepared for *The Making of Americans* there might have come an extended two or three-generation family chronicle such as *Buddenbrooks*. Her underlying structure is the history of the Hersland (Stein) and Dehring families, the arrival in America of the European grandparents and the gradual Americanization of their descendants. It has been a common theme, but in the case of *The Making of Americans* the author has used her material in accordance with her previously developed theory of spontaneous composition. Instead of controlled development, her collated notes served as points of reference for the uncontrolled reflections to which she gave free rein and which followed one another inexhaustibly. Such constant repetitions with their slight shifts of balance were, she claimed, a replica of human existence. As she explained it in one of her lectures: 'I began to get enormously interested in hearing how everybody said the same thing over and over again with infinite variations but over and over again until finally if you listened with great intensity you could hear it rise and fall and tell all that there was inside them, but not so much by the actual words they said or the thoughts they had but the movement of their thought and words endlessly the same and endlessly different.'

It is true that just as the term Man includes all men, so in that sense can every individual human being be included in *The Making of Americans*. For Gertrude Stein has described people by removing most of their characteristic features, leaving only generalities behind that might be considered as all people because they are equally no people. They become shadows without colour or depth, recurring endlessly—sometimes under one name, sometimes under another—as phantoms of the author's brain beneath which lie buried her emotions. The following paragraph is fairly typical of this abstraction of individuality:

'Mostly all of them were honest enough men and women, mostly among them there were not any bad men and women. Mostly they were honest enough working men and women and their children went to school and went on to be decent enough men and women to go on living as their families had always been living. As I have just been saying there were not very many of them that were not good enough men and women. A few of them came to a bad end before they got through with their living but mostly all of them were honest enough men and women and they had good enough children and mostly they all made enough by working to keep on and be honest enough in their daily living.'

This may in a general sense be considered a bare outline of all the immigrants that ever came to the United States, but there is little to it beyond the statement of fact. One learns nothing about the immigrants, and the fact itself is of no significance.

The Making of Americans is a static book of echoing phrases that go on and on for sentences and paragraphs and pages, recurring, fading away, until they are superseded by another series of thought waves. Certain phrases like 'independent-dependent', 'stupid being' and 'as I was saying', continue throughout the book. Gertrude Stein herself said there was no reason why *The Making of Americans* should ever come to an end. There is a certain vague time sequence: the grandparents do arrive in America, the children marry, and the grandchildren grow up. But we learn little or nothing that is fundamental about any of them. Page follows page with the same undulating verbiage, the same generalized repetitions that recoil on themselves. A fog of ennui hangs about this word-pile built up by the weak pen running across so many quires of paper through the long night hours. Later Gertrude Stein evolved several theories to justify herself, maintaining that *The Making of Americans* was an account of 'every individual man or woman who ever was or ever will be living.' She also maintained that the book's unique significance lay in its being written in what she called 'the continuous present'. 'A continuous present is a continuous present' is the way she defined this in the cant of her lecture manner. In *Composition as Explanation* she went on to explain: 'I made almost a thousand pages of a continuous present . . . . a continuous present and using everything and beginning again. There was an elaboration of the complexities of using everything and of a continuous present and of a beginning again and again and again.'

The 'continuous present', a Bergsonian echo of pre-war Paris, is a term that does not fit the time structure of *The Making of Americans* and has no application to its substance. In a book of such leaden uniformity almost any page will serve as an example:

'So then *as I was just saying* Martha was in her daily living and her daily feeling more of them the people in small houses near the Hersland family then than she was of any other daily living or daily feeling then. *As I was saying* she was with them often in the evening, *as I was saying* she was not then very interesting to any of them then. *As I was saying* the future which would be different for her in kind than the future of them made a separation between them in the things she was knowing with them and the things they were knowing among them, in the things she was feeling with them and the things they were feeling among them, in the things she was doing with them and the things they were doing among them, in the way she was interesting to them and the way they were interesting to each other among themselves then. *As I was saying* all there was of daily living and daily feeling in her then was of the daily feeling and daily living they had among them. *As I was saying* in a way she was separated from them, though all the living and feeling she had in her then was the living and feeling she had from them, by the future living that would be different in her living from the future living any of them would naturally be having.

'*As I was saying* she was then not really very interesting to any one. She might have been a little interesting a couple of evenings to Harry Brenner but she never really was interesting to him.

'*As I was saying* she was then of their daily living and their daily feeling, the poorer people near them, and she was with them very often in the evening. *As I was saying*, etc. . . .'

Mr. Sutherland professes to see in such recurring phrases a reduction of time to a simple present and the destruction of history and narrative sequence. At the same time he finds in *The Making of Americans* 'the essence of all human history'. In his comprehensive apologia he elaborates on Gertrude Stein's original explanation. 'As to its form', he writes, '*The Making of Americans* being so intensely of an interior time, must articulate that time as its primary dimension, not the dimensions of external narrative. It cannot rely on the conventional sequences or the habitual interest of external events and received ideas to sustain the expressions.'[1]

Some pages farther on he offers his own explanation of the book's significance: 'Within the paragraphs the relations of ideas, the syntactical relations, the succession of sentences, are made to move and cohere and balance, to have a conduct and a phrasing that repro-

[1] Donald Sutherland, *Gertrude Stein: A Biography of Her Work*, p. 59.

duce the specific pressure or dynamic balance of the experienced subject matter, whether it be a person, a type, an idea, a feeling or even an event. This can be seen in the following presentation of an event from the inside.

' "This one, and the one I am now beginning describing is Martha Hersland and this is a little story in the acting in her of her being in her very young living, this one was a very little one then and she was running and she was in the street and it was a muddy one and she had an umbrella that she was dragging and she was crying. 'I will throw the umbrella in the mud', she was saying, she was very little then, she was just beginning her schooling, 'I will throw the umbrella in the mud', she said and no one was near her and she was dragging the umbrella and bitterness possessed her, 'I will throw the umbrella in the mud', she was saying and nobody heard her, the others had run ahead to get home and they had left her, 'I will throw the umbrella in the mud' and there was desperate anger in her; 'I have throwed the umbrella in the mud', burst from her, she had thrown the umbrella in the mud and that was the end of it all in her. She had thrown the umbrella in the mud and no one heard her as it burst from her, 'I have throwed the umbrella in the mud', it was the end of all that to her." '[1]

The specific pressures and dynamic balance of the experienced subject to be found in the thin echoes of this childhood incident recorded in Gertrude Stein's hypnagogic prose do not lend themselves to definition. Mr. Sutherland has used his syntactical relations to conceal a poverty of thought that is apparent enough

[1] op. cit., p. 62.

when one compares his explanation with the quoted text. For *The Making of Americans* from cover to cover is unrelieved by any spark of creative vitality. It is an amorphous and infertile growth, the product of a trivial mind held in suspension. Only later when that mind chose to reveal itself in a series of autobiographies was its essential triviality clearly underscored.

The Making of Americans was written from notes and had the formal structure of the Stein family background. Its failure to communicate any total impression to the reader is not due to the individual sentences which though ponderous are comprehensible, but in the cumulative weight of unfocussed iteration. In her subsequent writings Gertrude Stein discarded her familial past, applying her technique of composition directly to individuals and objects. The former she called Portraits, the latter she collected in her next book, *Tender Buttons*. After a brief fixative period she would write down whatever words came into her head, disregarding both syntax and meaning, and without allowing conscious reflection to intervene.

She explained *Tender Buttons* as cubism applied to writing. In one of her American lectures she offered a further characteristic elucidation: 'In *Tender Buttons* I discovered everything then and its name, discovered it and its name . . . I described everything.' Carl Van Vechten has mentioned how Gertrude Stein liked to spend hours arranging and re-arranging boxes of buttons. Her book's title reflects this preoccupation. The things dealt with are the still-life impedimenta of her own home, arranged under the headings of Objects, Food and Rooms. She wrote

these descriptions at odd moments on scraps of paper
as the random thoughts came to her. Milk, for example,
she described as: 'Climb up in sight climb in the whole
utter needles and a guess a whole guess is hanging.
Hanging hanging.' Rhubarb was revealed as a 'susan
not susan not seat in bunch toys not wild and laughable
not in little places not on neglect and vegetable not in
fold coal age not please.'

It has been asserted that through this process of
transferring haphazard sequences of words to paper,
Gertrude Stein has revivified a moribund language,
shaken it out of its stale and outworn mould, re-
furbished it, removed the associative verdigris and
restored the word to its original new-minted bright-
ness. According to William Carlos Williams, she,
'having taken words to her choice, to emphasize
further what she had in mind had completely unlinked
them from their former relationships to sentences.
This was absolutely essential and unescapable.' Mr.
Julian Sawyer maintains that 'if the name of anything
or everything is dead, as Miss Stein has always rightly
contended, the only thing to do to keep it alive is to
rename it. And that is what Miss Stein did.' Mr. Sawyer
does not explain how anything dead can be kept alive,
nor enlarge on the revivifying effect of such examples
as those given to overcome the weight of such outworn
nouns as milk and rhubarb. Edith Sitwell, also
oppressed by the inert weight of inherited language,
would have it that 'Miss Stein is bringing back life to
our language by what appears, at first, to be
an anarchic process. First she breaks down the
predestined group of words, their sleepy familiar
habits; then she rebrightens them, examines their

texture and builds them into new and vital shapes.'

Such assertions are little more than ringing verbiage. The fact is, as I. A. Richards earlier pointed out in his *Principles of Literary Criticism*, 'words have no characters. None are either ugly or beautiful, intrinsically displeasing or delightful. Every word has instead a range of possible effects varying with the conditions into which it is received.'

Written extemporaneously as it was, *Tender Buttons* is a series of fragments any one of which is as typical as the next. Among Objects a sound is 'elephant beaten with candy and little pops and chews all bolts and reckless reckless rats, this is this.' 'A Carafe That Is A Blind Glass'—whatever that may be—becomes 'a kind in glass and a cousin, a spectacle and nothing strange a single hurt color and an arrangement in a system of pointing. All this and not ordinary, not unordered in not resembling. The difference is spreading.'

Eyeglasses are 'a color in shaving, a saloon is well placed in the centre of an alley.' As for food: 'Dining is west'; a cutlet, 'a blind agitation is manly an uttermost'.

Rooms are defined: 'All along the tendency to deplore the absence of more has not been authorized. It comes to mean that with burning there is that pleasant state of stupefaction. Then there is a way of earning a living. Who is man.' And so on.

Mr. Sutherland finds in *Tender Buttons*, in this 'great welter of what seems to be particularities and trivialities a "religious" attitude towards everything as simple existence. She', he goes on, referring to the author, 'said the change at this time was from feeling that everything was simply alike to feeling that everything was simply different, and that "different" was the constant intention of these works.'

What the 'religious' attitude is that can be discovered in the surface free-associations of *Tender Buttons* defies elucidation—in spite of such pseudo-technical jargon. Gertrude Stein called the book her 'first conscious struggle with the problem of correlating sight, sound and sense, and eliminating rhythm', although in fact *Tender Buttons* is neither a conscious effort nor a struggle, nor is there any correlation between sight, sense and sound. In the extracts already given, the words have been unquestionably unlinked from their meanings, but there is nothing either essential or inescapable in the resulting verbal kaleidoscope. Gertrude Stein defined her own peculiar attitude towards words with that complacent fatuity that is the most marked feature of her autobiographies. 'I found', she wrote, 'that any kind of book if you read it with glasses on and you use your glasses as a magnifying glass and so read word by word reading word by word makes the writing that is not anything be something.' Literally applied this would of course reduce all printed matter to a level at which Chaucer, Martin Tupper, Shakespeare, *The Adventures of Tarzan*, a school arithmetic and *Tender Buttons* would be of equal value.

Only an egotism reinforced by pathological naïvety could allow itself such a statement as the one about the glasses or Gertrude Stein's later remark that her grasp of the emotional distinction between paragraphs and sentences came to her through listening to her poodle drinking water. She once said in a candid moment that the difference between her writing and that of the insane was that one could go on reading her. In actual fact the writings of the insane are often more readable than *Tender Buttons*, although Gertrude Stein was right in drawing the parallel. For in the work of both there is the same incoherence of sense impressions the same assumption of super-human achievement, the same indifference as to the communicable result.

Contrary to superficial impressions Gertrude Stein is not a complicated writer. There is in such a work as *Tender Buttons*, as John Sparrow pointed out, simply an absence of meaning. The elementary fact to understand about Gertrude Stein is that she is incomprehensible because there is nothing to comprehend. It is no use for the reader to puzzle over definitions like the 'elephant beaten with candy' or 'a color in shaving'. There may have been psychological reasons for the author's using these particular phrases, but in themselves they mean nothing.

By the time Gertrude Stein reached her fortieth year *Three Lives* had been published privately, she had finished the manuscripts of *The Making of Americans* and *Tender Buttons*, and she was working on her *Portraits* in which she alternated between the repetitions of *The Making of Americans* and the word-fragments of *Tender Buttons*. Beyond her immediate circle she was still unknown.

In 1913 her *Portrait of Mabel Dodge at the Villa Curonia* which she had written while staying with Mrs. Dodge in Italy was printed in pamphlet form. The latter distributed it at large to her friends, and within the same year arranged to have it published in the American magazine, *Arts and Decoration*. Its appearance, accompanied by an explanatory article of Mrs.

Dodge's, brought Gertrude Stein's work for the first time to general public attention. The reaction was emphatic. In Gertrude Stein the smart set of pre-war intellectuals discovered an engaging enigma, a new literary sphinx that although it put no intelligible question did give something to talk about. Readers who could make little out of 'blankets are warmer in the summer and the winter is not lonely', etc., became intrigued nevertheless by the novelty.

According to Mrs. Dodge's article: 'In a large studio in Paris, hung with paintings by Renoir, Matisse and Picasso, Gertrude Stein is doing with words what Picasso is doing with paint. She is impelling language to induce new states of consciousness, and in doing so language becomes with her a creative art rather than a mirror of history.

'In her impressionistic writing she uses familiar words to create perceptions, conditions and states of being, never before quite consciously experienced. She does this by using words that appeal to her as having the meaning that they *seem* to have. She has taken the English language and, according to many people has mis-used it, or has used it roughly, uncouthly and brutally, or madly, stupidly and hideously, but by her method she is finding the hidden nature of nature.

'To present her impressions she chooses words for their inherent quality rather than for their accepted meaning.

'Her habit of working is methodical and deliberate. She always works at night in the silence and brings all her will power to bear upon the banishing of pre-conceived images. Concentrating upon the impression she has received and which she wishes to transmit, she suspends her selective faculty, waiting for the word or group of words that will perfectly interpret her meaning, to rise from her subconscious to the surface of her mind.

'Then and only then does she bring her reason to bear upon them, examining, weighing and gauging their ability to express their meaning.' . . .

This is an early example of the deceptive self-deceiving criticism that was later to become so common, with the emphasis on unidentifiable absolutes such as the nature of nature and the 'inherent' quality of words. As for 'perfectly interpreting the meaning', Mrs. Dodge wrote with more candour, twenty years later, that when Gertrude composed her *Portrait at the Villa Curonia* 'the symbolism had become so obscure that only by feeling it could one get the key to what she was saying'—or in plainer words that one could not get the key at all. Hutchins Hapgood who at this time had written about *Three Lives* in a vein similar to Mrs. Dodge's reflections, wrote again in 1939: 'My present feeling about her (Gertrude Stein's) work is quite different from what it was in those days long ago. Now, what seemed significant then, seems almost childishly idiotic, and yet there can be no doubt that her early work added something new and had an influence on other writers.'[1]

Such writing as the *Portrait of Mabel Dodge at the Villa Curonia* had snob appeal when the irrational was still an innovation. Gertrude Stein became a controversial figure, and through this process of sweeping defence and outraged attack she gained notoriety. At this time she began to demonstrate her showman's

[1] *A Victorian in the Modern World* (Harcourt, Brace & Co.).

instinct, her flair for publicity that was to become the dominant factor in creating the legend to grow up around her so lushly with the years. When *Life*, the old humorous magazine, printed a few parodies of her work she sent the editor some of her sketches, explaining that the originals were really much funnier than the imitations. The editor published them.

With the somewhat casual arrival from San Francisco of Miss Toklas at the rue de Fleurus and her permanent installation there the two Steins separated. Leo had no sympathy with his sister's literary innovations. Miss Toklas was merely the immediate cause. As he explained in a letter to Mabel Weeks in 1913: 'One of the greatest changes that has become decisive in recent times is the fairly definite "disaggregation" of Gertrude and myself. The presence of Alice was a godsend, as it enabled the thing to happen without any explosion. . . . Gertrude hungers and thirsts for *gloire*, and it was of course a serious thing for her that I can't abide her stuff and think it abominable. . . . Her artistic capacity is, I think, extremely small. I have just been looking over the Melanctha thing again. Gertrude's mind is as little nimble as a mind can be. She can only express herself elaborately by telling all at full length. The grammar and vocabulary and sentence structure of the three lives might have been different in a dozen ways without loss, provided that she had put down all she knows about the people concerned. It is the insistence on the facts that makes, to my thinking, the significance of the book. Well, Gertrude also wants to create a great and original form. I can't understand the *Portrait of Mabel Dodge*, but none the less I feel that I am not exceeding my reasonable privilege in thinking it damned nonsense. A portrait of a person that I know pretty intimately which conveys absolutely nothing to me, a far from inexperienced reader with no prejudices in the matter, seems to me to have something the matter with it.'

Twenty years later, looking back on their two careers, Leo Stein maintained that his sister had turned to writing jargon because she could not express herself effectively in English. She, however, and her apologists asserted that she had evolved a method of direct apprehension of reality, that in her portraits she had reached out to the essence of a person stripped of all accidental accretions and had achieved a four-dimensional portrait independent even of time.

Yet when one turns from such high claims to the actual portraits, one finds little more than a child's haphazard arrangement of alphabet blocks or the sing-song of counting-out rhymes—as in the *Portrait of Georges Hugnet*:

> George Genevieve Geronimo straightened it out
> without their finding it out.
> Grammar makes George in our ring which
> Grammar makes George in our ring.
> Grammar is as disappointed not is as grammar is
> disappointed.
> Grammar is not as Grammar is as disappointed.
> George is in our ring. Grammar is not is dis-
> appointed. In are ring.
> George Genevieve in are ring.

To Mr. Sutherland such finger exercises, far from being merely sterile patterns, are a charismatic revelation. 'This terrific attempt', he writes, 'to express a concentrated knowing of a living thing while foregoing discourse and melody and movement in space may, while perfectly intellectual in intention and method and not mystic, be compared to the exquisite isolated energy, the ecstacy of Plotinus's mind approaching the vision of God.'[1]

A further example of Gertrude's Stein's portraiture, this time of a well-known figure, is contained in the *Portrait of T. S. Eliot* that concludes :

> He said enough.
> Enough said.
> He said enough.
> Enough said.
> Enough said.
> He said enough.
> He said enough.
> Enough said.
> He said enough.

Not only wool and woolen silk and silken not only silk and silken wool and woolen not only wool and woolen silk and silken not only silk and silken wool and woolen not only wool and woolen silk and silken not only silk and silken not only wool and woolen not only wool and woolen not only silk and silken not only silk and silken not only wool and woolen.

It would indeed take much ingenuity on Mr. Sutherland's part to demonstrate what concentrated knowing of the subject is shown here. The portrait, as Leo Stein said of that of Mabel Dodge, contains nothing identi-

[1] *Gertrude Stein*, op. cit., p. 147.

fiable with Mr. Eliot, tells us nothing about him. It could be applied with equal appropriateness to any other individual or object in the Stein catalogue.

The difficulty with practitioners like Gertrude Stein and such transcendental theorists as Mr. Sutherland and M. Jolas is that they have failed to grasp what words really are. For words are merely sounds, modifications of primitive vocables, that have over the centuries become symbolic approximations of the apprehended objects of the external world in their relationship to ourselves. Once their symbolic value is altered, the point of reference is lost. Δένδρον, arbor, arbre, Baum, tree, are the conventional signs for what the dictionary defines as 'a perennial plant with a single woody self-supporting stem'. Change these symbols arbitrarily—as the Stein apologists suggest, because of the feeling that they are stale or outworn—and understanding between individuals breaks down.

The basic function of language is to communicate. With each generation our speech alters to a degree both in pronunciation and meaning as it reflects changes in the conditions of life, but its progress is evolutionary rather than revolutionary. With the appearance of literature the canons of language tend to become more fixed. Latin at the greatest extent of the Roman Empire had stabilized itself. The requirements for the birth of a new language are social convulsions and widespread illiteracy. Only from the ruins of the Empire, when kings themselves could not read, did the new Romance languages emerge. It was not a conscious effort that created French, Spanish, Provencal, and Italian, but the stark and urgent necessity of communication that forced the barbarians to evolve new forms out of the literate tongue superimposed by an alien governing class on their crude native speech. This brutal process had nothing in common with any precious playing with words by a handful of pedantic intellectuals.

To those who believe with M. Jolas that European languages have exhausted their possibilities, it would seem both more logical and more fruitful to turn to an artifact language such as Esperanto rather than to lapse into a contrived obscurity. Esperanto is an inter-language, understood by several million people in various parts of the world, but with its epics and lyrics still unwritten. It is simple to learn and easy to compre-hend. Esperantists are by the nature of their interests literate and above average in intelligence. They are, it would seem, an ideal audience only waiting for their poets to appear.

The difficulty with Esperanto, however, is that it is obviously communicable, and communicable thought subjects itself to the ordinary laws of understanding and criticism. On the other hand the great advantage of incommunicability—so apparent in the pages of *Transition* and the works of Gertrude Stein—is that when once granted its initial premise it is not subject to criticism. At its first appearance it is as startling as some lone sphinx in the middle of the desert, though after the desert is populated with large numbers of similar sphinxes this effect is lost. Gertrude Stein well understood the publicity value of a sustained enigma and the advantage of being first on the scene. In her old age she admitted ingenuously: 'They ask me why an author like myself can become popular. It is very easy everybody keeps saying and writing what anybody feels they are understanding and so they get tired of that, anybody can get tired of anything and so they do not know it but they get tired of feeling they are understanding and so they take pleasure in having something that they feel they are not understanding.'

Although Gertrude Stein was always to maintain that *The Making of Americans* was her greatest piece of work, the manner of *Tender Buttons* was the one she preferred in her middle period, in the portraits and what she called her plays and landscapes. There were echoes of her earlier repetitive style in a few of the portraits and a continuation of it in the posthumously published *Two*, but this method necessitated following a fairly rigid outline that she now found irksome, as she herself said 'one had to be remembering'. It was easier to adopt the free word-play manner of *Tender Buttons* that could be scribbled down at odd moments without regard for sequence. Her plays were written in this manner, although except for the gratuitous use of the directives 'Scene' and 'Act' they are not plays at all but merely random offshoots of her indifferent fancy.[1] In one of her American lectures she gave a typical account of how she began to write plays.

'I had just come home from a pleasant dinner party and I realized then as anybody can know that something is always happening. . . . So naturally what I wanted to do in my play was what everybody did not always know or tell. By everybody I do of course include myself by always I do of course include myself.

[1] See Rosalind S. Miller's *Gertrude Stein: Form and Intelligibility* (The Exposition Press, 1949), p. 62. 'According to Miss Stein's usage any piece of writing, whether it is an individual portrait or just a digression in a larger prose work, whose paragraphs or sections are divided by the insertions of the term "act" or "scene" is a play.'

'And so I wrote *What Happened, A Play*. . . . in short to make a play the essence of what happened.'

Where she had divided the fragments of *Tender Buttons* under the headings of Objects, Food and Rooms, she divided her plays into conventionally labelled scenes and acts. There, however, the convention ended, for these play fragments contained no dialogue and lacked any time sequence. Two short paragraphs, for example became the fifth act of *What Happened*:

Act V
(Two.)

A regret a single regret makes a door way. What is a door way, a doorway is a photograph. What is a photograph, a photograph is a sight and a sight is always a sight of something. Very likely there is a photograph that gives color if there is then there is that color does not change any more than it did when there was much more use for photography.

Other plays are even more abbreviated. The whole four acts of a play called *Counting Her Dresses* contain less than thirty words:

Act I.
When she did not see me.
I saw them again.
I did not like it.

Act II.
I count her dresses again.

Act III.
Can you draw a dress.

Act IV.
In a minute.

According to her own explanation, Gertrude Stein by writing plays stripped of dialogue, action, suspense and characterization uncovered their primal quality. This quality, she maintained, was best typified by a landscape. As she wrote in her autobiography, 'a landscape is such a natural arrangement for a battlefield or a play that one must write plays'. As with most of her theories, when they are applied to the matter at hand they result in no further clarification, nor—as the untoward reference to the battlefield suggests—was there any such intention on the author's part. She defined her most widely-known play, *Four Saints in Three Acts*, in a similar manner:

'In *Four Saints* I made the Saints the landscape. All the saints that I made and I made a number of them because after all a great many pieces of things are in a landscape all these saints together made my landscape.'

Four Saints appeared first in *Transition* in June 1929 as—by this time—one of Gertrude Stein's conventional pieces. Since the founding of the magazine her work had been published in it regularly. The editor, M. Jolas, used to print with a certain coyness in his list of contributors: 'And Gertrude Stein sends us what she writes and when she writes and she is pleased and we are pleased.' In 1928 he had written pontifically: 'In structurally spontaneous composition in which words are grouped rhythmically she succeeds in giving us her mathematics of the word, clear, primitive and beautiful.' The irony of this becomes apparent a few years later in *Transition's* special supplement devoted to denouncing Gertrude Stein.

Gertrude Stein was not a believer and had only the most superficial knowledge of hagiology. In *Four*

Saints she wrote ostensibly of Saint Teresa and Saint Ignatius. The idea of writing about Saint Ignatius came to her from a Spanish porcelain group she saw in a Parisian art dealer's window, the central figure of which she erroneously assumed to be Saint Ignatius. She found the inspiration for her Saint Teresa while looking at the picture of a little girl dressed as a nun in a commercial photographer's shop. These two conceptions she combined with a dozen other saints, paying no attention to their actual histories.

In spite of the nomenclature there is nothing in *Four Saints* that illuminates any facet of the life either of Saint Teresa or Saint Ignatius. It is written without fore or hind-thought in the author's now familiar method of composition, as if after receiving her inspiration from the porcelain group and the child's photograph she had gone home and let the words drift onto the paper. In itself *Four Saints* would not merit any more attention than the numerous little proto-plays beginning with *What Happened*. However, because of its spectacular stage production, *Four Saints* became more widely known and disputed than any other of Gertrude Stein's pieces. Among other things it demonstrated her old cunning in drawing attention to herself. Such a combination of non-meaning with religious themes was bound to arouse controversy. Her selection of an all-Negro cast, though without literary significance, was a master stroke of publicity.

Above all, *Four Saints* was lavishly and beautifully produced. The settings and costumes were of a baroque opulence. Both Saint Teresas—for there were two of them—wore scarlet gowns and adaptations of cardinals' hats. Saint Ignatius was dressed in a flowing green robe. The singers were melodious, the choreography lively, and Virgil Thomson's derivative music had a sugar-coated charm that made it easy to disregard the meaningless libretto:

> Four Saints two at a time have to have to have to
> have to.
> Have to have to have to.
> Two saints four at a time.
> Have to have to at a time.
> Four saints have to have to have at a time.
> The difference between saints forget-me-nots and
> mountains have to have to have to have to at a time,
> etc.

According to Mr. Sutherland, Gertrude Stein's theatre is visual and spectacular rather than dramatic. In a more limited sense than he intended he is correct, for in its stage version *Four Saints* was a spectacle, a kind of choral ballet. Whatever interest it carried for the audience was not contained in the author's words but due to the efforts of the stage designer, the choreographer and Virgil Thomson. A reviewer of the 1952 revival of *Four Saints* wrote of his 'recurrent feeling of impatience over the dedication of so much artistic effort to a piece of sublime gibberish'. It is an apt enough summing-up, his qualifying use of sublime being merely an indication of his uneasiness in affronting yesterday's *avant-garde* opinion.

There is no need of any qualifying adjective for:

> 'My country 'tis of thee sweet land of liberty of thee
> I sing.
> Saint Therese something like that.

Saint Therese something like that.
Saint Therese would and would and would.
Saint Therese something like that.
Saint Therese, etc.

or the iteration of:

Saint Therese seated and not standing half and half
of it and not half and half of it seated and not standing
surrounded and not seated and not seated and not
standing and not surrounded not surrounded not not,
not seated not seated not seated not surrounded not
seated and Saint Ignatius standing standing not seated
Saint Therese not standing not standing and Saint
Ignatius not standing standing surrounded as if in once
yesterday. In place of situations.

Gertrude Stein explained her play in one of those
explanations that fall just short of explaining. 'A saint',
she wrote in her autobiography, 'a real saint never does
anything, a martyr does something but a really good
saint does nothing, and so I wanted to have Four
Saints who did nothing and I wrote *Four Saints in
Three Acts* and they did nothing and that was everything. . . . That is what a saint or a doughboy should
do, they should do nothing, they should move some
and they did move some and they did nothing and it
was very satisfying.'

This bland assertion that the essence of a saint or a
soldier is to do nothing is merely another example of
the author's pretentious efforts to justify logically her
verbal arpeggios. Here is the end of Act I, Scene II:

Let Lucy Lily Lily Lucy Lucy let Lucy Lucy Lily Lily Lily Lily Lily let Lily Lucy Lucy let Lily. Let Lucy Lily.

The effect is similar to that of a person with no knowledge of music who strikes a series of three or four notes on the piano with one finger, making up various sequences without regard for harmony— incidentally a private amusement of Gertrude Stein's.

One of the idiosyncracies of Gertrude Stein's work, of which there are innumerable examples in *Four Saints*, is the use of internal rhyme in progressions of jingles such as children use, where one word suggests another almost ad infinitum. Sometimes again an actual counting out rhyme is used, as in the second act:

One two three four five six seven all good children go to heaven some are good and some are bad one two three four five six seven.
Scene eight. To wait.
Scene one. And begun.
Scene two. To and to.
Scene three. Happily be.
Scene four. Attached or.
Scene five. Sent to derive.
Scene six. Let it mix.
Scene seven. Attached eleven.
Scene eight. To wait.

Scene nine of the third act begins:

Letting pin in letting let in let in in in let in let in wet in wed in dead in dead wed lead in lead wed dead in dead in let in wed in said in led wed dead wed dead

said led led said wed dead wed dead led in led in wed
in wed in said in wed in led in said in dead in dead wed
said led led said wed dead in.

These straggling sequences that march about the
page like an army minus its leaders are a familiar con-
cealing device. There are in Gertrude Stein's middle
writings no clues to her personality. Long ago she
had revealed herself and she did not intend to do so
again. So consistently did she bar the door to her own
feelings that she 'forgot' about her first book, nor
when it came to light did she allow it to be published.
The rhymes without reason of the Lucy Lilies and the
dead-wed-leds are a magical gesture, a banning of the
active thought beneath the surface of her mind.

In the decade following the publication of the
Portrait of Mabel Dodge, Gertrude Stein developed into
the priestess of a cult. Her little house in the rue de
Fleurus became a port of call for the generation of
post-war expatriates. The less secure members of that
exodus found her established, self-assured and assur-
ing. With the years she had acquired a re-inforcing
physical bulk and with it a massive presence. Powers
Hapgood returning after a long interval noted with
surprise that she had come to look like an oriental god
'with the young and faithful kneeling at her feet'.
Osbert Sitwell described her about this time as monumental, having the eagle features of a Red Indian
warrior. Indeed she resembled most the staring
profile of a Roman emperor, and like an emperor kept
the same egocentric attitude towards the external
world. Leo Stein, who could never take his sister

seriously as a literary phenomenon, held that she had succeeded merely by the weight of her insistence over the years, the way drops of water finally make an impression even on stone.

To the faithful her writing was an enigma not to be questioned but to be treated with awe. There was something undeniably attractive and impressive in that assured bulky figure holding forth from her chair in the rue de Fleurus studio with the Cézannes and the Matisses and the Picassos lining the walls. Gertrude Stein became a symbol, and the young men flocked to her, the celebrities and the future celebrities. These were of course overwhelmingly outnumbered by the would-be celebrities, the creative hopefuls who would in the end after much bitter searching and without her help resign themselves to their lack of talent. But at the beginning of a young writer's career, when he had come third-class to Paris with his half-finished auto-biographical novel in his valise, that exciting tele-phoned summons from Miss Toklas was his first outward sign of approval and success. He had arrived.

A generation later Van Wyck Brooks summed up these young men: 'She (Gertrude Stein) admitted them to the magic circle on which the world's limelight fell and of which, wonderful to say, they became members, while her positive note was reassuring at a time when all values seemed insecure, when old standards and habits of thought had apparently vanished. What did her egomania matter or even the megalomania that no one challenged in this circle of youthful adorers. . . . She could play the pontiff as she liked to the young men who sat at her feet, intriguing among themselves for her sovereign good will, even when they were well aware that, wherever her own interests were concerned, she was as coldly shrewd as any horse-trader. . . . At the little court in the rue de Fleurus they all felt moreover, what Leo Stein said, "when one is doing the latest thing, one can feel at least a little bit important." [1] Gertrude Stein was in fact a forceful domineering shrewd old woman who like a strong-minded medium was able to assert her will over the members of her circle.

Her intransigeance in the use of words had a publicity value that she knew how to capitalize on. Her countrymen—most of whom had never read a line of hers—were beginning to laugh at the mention of her name, and she was the subject of jokes and limericks. As long as they remembered the name she did not mind. For her the important thing was to be noticed. Whether the result was fame or notoriety made little difference. People were becoming aware of her. Long ago when she had sat shyly in the shadow of her more brilliant brother she had wanted above all to cut a figure in the world, to be not just a fat woman in eccentric clothes walking through Montmartre but the enigmatic celebrity whom tourists would point out as Gertrude Stein.

With that touch of clairvoyance she possessed and that made her originally sense the currents of anti-reason on which she had built up her reputation, she now sensed—as in the more violent patterns of the surrealists—that she might become eclipsed and out-moded. So after a lapse of thirty years she took up her pen with conscious intent and in six weeks wrote the volume of reminiscences to which she gave the ingenu-

[1] *The Confident Years* 1885-1915 (Dent, 1952), p. 569.

ous title of *The Autobiography of Alice B. Toklas.*

As she admitted later, she had always wished for a wider recognition than the limited scale of the *Transatlantic Review* and *Transition*. She wanted to see herself in the pages of the *Atlantic Monthly* and the mass-distributed *Saturday Evening Post.* For the sake of that wider audience she had always anticipated, she returned to a conventional manner of writing, willingly sacrificing the esoteric world of the little reviews in the process. With the serial appearance of *Alice B. Toklas* in the *Atlantic Monthly*, Gertrude Stein for the first time reached the suburban intelligentzia.

Writing of herself in the third person, through the fiction of Miss Toklas, she came out from behind the barricade of words she had erected. These gossipy sometimes jejune recollections, in spite of their carried-over repetitions and false-naïve manner, have a sprightliness about them that is a welcome relief to what has gone before. *Alice B. Toklas* is easy to read. Time does move, events occur, now and then the author pays off old scores—often amusingly enough as in the cases of Hemingway and Matisse. It is as straight a kind of writing as she could muster. Beneath its surface ripples it gives her away, exposes her shallowness, her flaccid impervious mind.

What is apparent here, what becomes even more apparent in her later autobiographical volumes, is her isolation from the world she lived in. Wars and depressions, the cataclysms of our times, never penetrated into the comfortable isolated existence she had contrived for herself. What she lacked basically was any standard of judgement. Her mental blindness allowed her to compare her patterned vocables, from which as Mr. Sparrow remarked meaning had taken wing, to Shakespeare, Homer and the Bible—or as in *Alice B. Toklas* to state flatly that she was the only one in her time in English literature, that she always knew it and now she said it. Wars for her were merely 'nice' and 'not nice'. There is no apparent relation between such sombre battles as Ypres and the Somme, and the two fantastic women in Red Cross uniforms and green veils driving round the south of France in a Model-T Ford, so outlandish in appearance, according to their friend Tristan Tzara, that they drew crowds when they stopped.

Although *Alice B. Toklas* has interest in the same way that Mrs. Dodge's butterfly memoirs often make interesting reading, neither persons nor events really become alive. One does not relive imaginatively Gertrude Stein's experiences, there is no moving sense of continuity with the past such as one finds for example in the autobiographical volumes of Osbert Sitwell.

For M. Jolas the appearance of *Alice B. Toklas* was a betrayal to which he replied indignantly in his supplement, *Testimony Against Gertrude Stein*. 'There is a unanimity of opinion', he wrote, 'that she (Gertrude Stein) had no understanding of what was really happening around her, that the mutation of ideas beneath the surface of the more obvious contacts and classes of personalities during that period escaped her entirely. Her participation in the genesis and developments of such movements as Fauvism, Cubism, Dada, Surrealism, Transition, etc., was never ideologically intimate and, as M. Matisse states, she has presented the epoch without taste and without relation to reality.'

According to Madame Jolas's testimony, 'Miss Stein seemed to be experimenting courageously, and while my husband was never enthusiastic about her solution of language, still it was a very personal one, and language being one of his chief preoccupations, she obviously belonged with us. Her final capitulation to a Barnumesque publicity none of us could foresee.'

The Dadaist poet, M. Tzara, after recalling the green veils of World War I and un-gently referring to Miss Toklas in quotation marks as 'secretary', wrote Gertrude Stein off for good: 'Underneath the "Baby" style, which is pleasant enough when it is a question of simpering at the interstices of envy, it is easy to discern such a really coarse spirit, accustomed to the artifices of the lowest literary prostitution, that I cannot believe it necessary for me to insist on the presence of a clinical case of megalomania.'

For the *Transition* group Gertrude Stein had committed the unpardonable offence. She had made herself clear. Consistency is on the side of the Jolases. As Stephen Spender remarked, if she had been justified in her experiments, if she had been on the right track in the first place, what excuse did she then have for changing her whole manner of expression and reverting to the conventions she had repudiated? The answer lies not in her artistic but in her practical self. She had extracted everything she could from the closed circles and the little reviews. With *Alice B. Toklas* she became a best-seller. Those not of the élite who had heard so much of Gertrude Stein through the years now found to their relief that they could understand her. From *Transition* she moved on to the book clubs.

In 1934, the year after the publication of the Toklas

book and on the strength of her new popularity and wider public, Gertrude Stein returned to America for a series of lectures. It was a deftly organized tour, managed with the maximum of publicity. She arrived in New York suitably bizarre in appearance, to be given the kind of welcome reserved for Hollywood stars, aviators and channel swimmers. Holding interviews attended by as many reporters as at a presidential conference, on view in the news reels, written up on the front pages of the metropolitan dailies, she was a sensational billing—the return of the Enigma. Her opinions were asked and quoted on a variety of irrelevant subjects, her voice was recorded as she recited 'Pigeons on the grass, alas', from *Four Saints*.

She appeared like a swami at various colleges and universities throughout the United States, lecturing with a spectacular positiveness that seemed to mute her audiences. It was a good act. Crowds came to see and listen to her—out of curiosity, intellectual snobbery, passing interest, amusement. She had presence and she entertained them all, juggling with words, sending her audiences away again never quite sure what or whether they had understood. For if one were in a receptive mood and not too critical, one might puzzle over what seemed novel and profound thoughts, such as for example her pronouncement that sentences were not emotional and paragraphs were—a fact that was revealed to her, so she wrote in *Alice B. Toklas*, through listening to her poodle drinking water. Only later, in this and other statements, would one come to realize that Gertrude Stein had again provided a key of her own contriving that did not fit anything. 'English Literature', she announced, 'has been with us a long time, quite a few hundred years, and during all that time it has had a great deal to do and also it has a great deal not to do.' She could remark with an air of discovery that 'prose and poetry are not at all alike. They are completely different. Poetry is, I say, essentially a vocabulary just as prose is essentially not.' For her familiar bit of doggerel, 'a rose is a rose is a rose ', which she fitted as a motto to some of her books, she claimed that in it the rose was red for the first time in English poetry for a hundred years. In her lecture on the genesis of *The Making of Americans* she made the same cosmic claims for her work that have been regularly advanced for some of the century's better-known obscurantist writers. Again it is the illusion —though the sincerity of such claims is always an open question—that the problem of life and human destiny can be solved by a re-arrangement of words. 'I was sure,' she said, describing the repetitive sequences of *The Making of Americans*, 'that in a kind of way the enigma of the universe could in this way be solved. That after all description is explanation, and if I went on and on enough I could describe every individual human being that could possibly exist. I did proceed to do so as much as I could.'

Of *Tender Buttons* and her work after *The Making of Americans* she declared categorically: 'The strict discipline that I had given myself, the absolute refusal of never using a word that was not an exact word all through the *Tender Buttons* and what I may call the early Spanish and Geography and Play period finally resulted in things like Susie Asado and Preciosilla, etc., in an extraordinary melody of words and a melody of excitement in knowing that I had done this thing.' As an example she gave the extract:

> Sweet sweet sweet sweet sweet tea.
>   Susie Asado.
> Sweet sweet sweet sweet sweet tea.
>   Susie Asado.

A better example might have been from *Preciosilla* with its babbling echoes of the nursery rhyme, *Star Bright*:

> Not so dots large diamonds bright, diamonds in the in the light, diamonds light diamonds door diamonds hanging to be four, two four, all before, this bean, lessly, all most, a best, willow, rest, a green guest, go go go go go go, go. Go, go. Not guessed. Go, go.'

The claim that such word play has any connection with intellectual discipline and exactitude is, however, much like finding literary enlightenment in a dog's slurping.

In every sense, including the financial one, Gertrude Stein's American tour was an enormous success. That same year in the wake of the lectures the world première of *Four Saints* took place in Hartford, Connecticut.

In Gertrude Stein's second autobiographical volume, *Everybody's Autobiography*, which appeared in 1937 and in which she discarded the fictive Miss Toklas and wrote in the first person, she gave an account of her American tour. The lionizing aspects of it had delighted her. 'It is very nice to be a celebrity', she wrote, 'a celebrity who can decide who they want to meet and say so and they come or do not come as you want them. I never imagined that would happen to me to be a celebrity like that but it did and when it did I liked it but all that will come later.' Throughout the book the general run of her comments are on the same level of false naïvety, though she gives more insight into the workings of her mind than in the Toklas auto-biography. Again as in that first volume one is struck by her imperviousness. During the turbulent decade that began with an economic collapse, saw the shift of political power in the United States and the rise of Hitler in Europe, and ended in war, she was capable of writing about the depression: 'It is curious very curious and yet not at all unreasonable that when there is a great deal of unemployment and misery you can never find anybody to work for you. It is funny that but that is the way it is.'

According to her view of French politics, 'of course in France you never know it may be anything it might be another republic or soviets not so likely red very red or rather pink often quite pink, a king not so likely but perhaps a king not very likely a Bourbon or Orleans king but barely possible, just now more likely just a prince some prince about whom nobody is thinking!' The bitter political riots of the last years of the Third Republic were for her merely a spectacle. 'Every evening when I was walking I was watching them gathering and one evening a woman next to me said we do not see anything, no not much I said and she said but if we climbed up something, in a French street there is always something to climb on and I said yes we might then see something yes she said but if anything was happening and we were on something it might be more dangerous than if we did not climb up on something yes I said and she said we had better stay where we are and I agreed with this thing.'

Everybody's Autobiography is in a sense a summing up of the author's beliefs, habits and tastes. By now the reader is almost used to finding her describing herself and Einstein as the two creative minds of the century. Yet for such a mind her amusements were rather extraordinary. She would sit for hours playing the piano with one finger, as she explained 'always on the white keys I do not like black keys and never two notes struck by the same hand at the same time because I do not like chords.' Her favourite musical composition was *The Trail of the Lonesome Pine* and she enjoyed singing it and playing it over and over again on the phonograph. And she admitted that she read only the cheapest detective and adventure stories. In her visit to the United States she was most impressed when she passed through Marion, Ohio, finding it one of the three or four outstanding moments of her life—this because of the town's connection with Warren G. Harding and the book, *The President's Daughter*, allegedly by his mistress. This meretricious ghost-written volume she considered 'one of the best descriptions of small town life in America that has been written', just as she thought that *Merton of the Movies* was 'the best book about twentieth-century American youth that has yet been done'.

That last interval before the war she spent alternating between Paris and her country home at Bilignin, arranging buttons, ordering tailored coats for her poodles, reading Gene Stratton Porter and books on fortune telling, and occasionally writing in her old mesmerized manner lest any critic imply she had abandoned it. The war took her by surprise. In *The Winner Loses* she wrote of its beginning: 'And then there was another Sunday and we were in Beon again that Sunday, and Russia came into the war and Poland was smashed, and I did not care about Poland, but it did frighten me about France—oh dear, that was another Sunday.'

She remained in the country during the war years, moving from Bilignin to Belley, keeping a record from month to month that was afterward published as *Wars I Have Seen*. Although she lived in Occupied France she was not molested by the Germans, nor, being in the country, did she suffer from any shortage of food. Her chief complaint during the years was of the lack of dental floss.

In the incidental details of the German occupation, *Wars I Have Seen* often has considerable interest, particularly in the final section when the American troops appear. Yet against the sweep of world events and the devastation of Europe her pre-occupations with food and dental floss, her garulous crotchety thinkings-aloud, take on for the reader an infuriating quality. She can prattle on about the war as inconsequentially as she did about sentences and paragraphs. 'Of course there are a good many times when there is no war just as there are a good many times when there is a war. To be sure when there is a war the years are longer that is to say the days are longer the months are longer the years are much longer but the weeks are shorter that is what makes a war.'

The tragedy of the war produced almost no effect

on her. The pages of *Wars I Have Seen* are scattered
with insubstantial figures, Germans, Maquis, collabora-
tors, and Vichy officials, that appear vaguely like so
many underexposed photographic negatives. The
defeat of France in 1940 seemed almost a game to her.
'In a way', she wrote, 'that is what makes it nice about
the French. In one war they upset the Germans by
resisting unalterably steadily and patiently for four
years, in the next war they upset them just as much by
not resisting at all and going under completely in six
weeks. Well that is what makes them changeable
enough to create styles.'

According to her view Marshal Pétain saved France
and by saving France defeated Germany. For her the
most extraordinary of all extraordinary things that
happened was the shortage of motor transportation for
the local German officers. Watching them, immobilized
as she was in Belley, she looked back wistfully to the
First World War when she and Alice, veiled and
uniformed, careened about the south of France in their
Model-T. That war was 'a nice war, a real war, a
regular war, a commenced and an ended war.'

At Belley she read the prophecies of Sainte Odile and
waited and hoped for the Americans to arrive 'with
shoes and stockings and dental floss'. Honey as a war
substitute for sugar could make her almost philo-
sophical: 'It's funny about honey, you always eat honey
during a war, so much honey, there is no sugar, there
never is sugar during a war, the first thing to disappear
is sugar, after that butter, but butter can always be had
but not sugar, no not sugar so during a war you always
eat quantities of honey, really more honey than you
used to eat sugar, and you find honey so much better

than sugar, better in itself and better in apple sauce, in all desserts so much better and then peace is upon us and no one eats honey any more, they find it too sweet and too cloying and too heavy, it was like this in the last war '14-'18 and it is like this in this war, wars are like that, it is funny but wars are like that.'

By 1943 she found it vexing to have to burn coal instead of wood, and although they had enough to eat, 'butter and cheese, and bread, white bread and fish and meat and vegetables and cake and honey and plenty of it', the two things they seemed to miss most were rice and orange marmalade. But 'life is like that and appetites are like that'. What was most annoying was not to be able to go out and buy something when one had the money, 'well of course it is the worst of all, that it is is the worst of all'.

In the same way her re-action to the D-Day an-nouncement was bounded by the limits of her personal comfort. 'To-day is the landing', she could jot down, 'and we heard Eisenhower tell us he was here they were here and just yesterday a man sold us ten packages of Camel cigarettes, glory be, and we are singing glory hallelujah, and feeling very nicely. . . .' The next day she wrote: 'To-night the Americans have just had a victory and are going to take Cherbourg and that is a pleasure. To be sure in the middle ages they did not have a wireless and although it was threatened that they would take them away from us they did not and now it would be rather late for it to happen and I do like to hear their American voices.'

The departure of the Germans and the arrival of the Americans—even though the latter event moved her deeply—she still chronicled in this juvenile manner as if she were a little girl rushing home to tell her mother what she had seen. She could write of the last days of the German occupation: 'We all hoped they would leave and that would be very comfortable for everybody and they would like to leave but Hitler likes everybody to stay where they are until they are all killed, he likes it like that, so I suppose even these few will stay until they are all killed so that now the railroad is not working any more there is no use in staying but their orders are to stay anyway.'

Beyond the superficial impressions set down in this rigmarole is a child's failure to grasp the adult significance of events. When the first American troops appeared she went to meet them. 'I said in a loud voice are there any Americans here and three men stood up and they were Americans God bless them and we were pleased. We held each other's hands and we patted each other and we sat down together and I told them who we were, and they knew, I always take it for granted that people will know who I am at the same time at the last moment I kind of doubt, but they knew, of course they knew.'

In her latter 'sixties Gertrude Stein had lost the massive bearing of her middle years. By the war's end she was a bent and shrunken woman who no doubt appeared rather pathetic to the troops as she first welcomed them. The good-natured Americans liked this crackpot flag-waving old woman who embraced them like a grandmother and whom they soon learned to call Gertie. She, an American woman, had stood up under the German occupation, and for that they respected her, imagining the terror of those years. That in Belley she had endured little beyond a shortage of dental floss and marmalade was no reflection of theirs.

Among the American troops this positive belligerently-patriotic old woman was a phenomenon that the army looked on with pleased indulgence. She was humoured, driven about in jeeps, flown to Frankfurt like a Very Important Person, entertained and entertaining in turn. She was a relief, as much of a diversion as any USO film comedian. Back in her Paris flat after the armistice she was visited by soldiers literate and illiterate. A few were interested in her writings. The rest came because they had heard of her, because it was the thing to do, because the others were coming. An illustrated weekly ran a series of pictures about her, surrounded by the men in uniform for whom she had become one of the sights of Paris.

The soldiers for the most part cared neither for her pictures nor her writings—if they were even aware of such things. They were interested in her as a talkative dominating old woman whose positive manner gave them many a laugh. She in turn reacted to these young men as if she were somehow trying to recapture her own American youth. As a result of her contact with the troops she wrote a short book, *Brewsie and Willie*, about American soldiers as she imagined she understood them. It is the most intensely felt piece she had written since *Things As They Are*. What she wanted to do was to grasp the speech of the common soldier and through it transmit a message to her fellow countrymen that she felt was in a sense her summing up.

What she succeeded in doing was merely to express the sterility of her own mind. *Brewsie and Willie* in its message is an inconsequent little tract against industrialism. England, as her sad example and warning, is a poor country now 'because it went industrial and the people lost their pep they went employee-minded and they manufactured more than they could use and they speeded it up, and they went bust'. Her solution is for the soldiers to 'stall' going home until there is another depression and then they can all go back and start little businesses of their own in the ruins of industrialism. 'Don't that listen good?' one of her pasteboard soldiers remarks.

Her soldiers are phantoms. She understood neither their thoughts nor their talk. Her Brewsie is an illiterate Werther rather than an infantryman. 'Oh dear', he remarks at one point as if he were wringing his hands, 'I guess you boys better go away I might just begin to cry and I'd better be alone. I am a G.I. and perhaps we better all cry, it might do us good crying sometimes does.' Through him Gertrude Stein can philosophize about the post-war era: 'Oh my good gracious, oh my good gracious and no worries, my good gracious. I just could kind of just cry when I think we all got to scratch around and worry, worry and scratch around, and then those bills, pay everything on the instalment plan, and coming in and coming in, oh dear, sometimes I just burst out crying in my sleep, 1 am older than you boys, you dont know, I could just burst out crying.'

She wished to capture the essence of these uniformed men who flocked to see her. But she was locked within herself. The soldiers were incomprehensible to her. She could not even catch the rhythm of their speech, and her final message was no more than the superficial reflections of a rentier. When she spoke in her own person, as she did at the end of *Brewsie and Willie*, her last words were merely a series of commonplaces on the American way.

There have been several books of Gertrude Stein's published since her death, most of them consisting of material left over from her pre-autobiographical period. However, in the posthumous *Last Operas and Plays*, among the brief word sequences she called plays, there is one actual short play written in conventional stage form, called *Yes Is For A Very Young Man*. Though of no particular interest in itself, it has considerable interest in the way it reflects on the author. As in the autobiographies, Gertrude Stein by returning to a discarded convention has subjected herself to conventional criticism. And as the meaning becomes clear so do the limitations of the mind behind the piece. *Four Saints* and the other landscape plays were written deliberately out of focus. The characters in *Yes Is For A Very Young Man* speak comprehensibly enough—though in the rambling manner of *Alice B. Toklas*—and the action is focussed on the French resistance movement.

The play was written under the impact of the liberation of France, but its basic inspiration goes back to the author's childhood and to the melodramas of the 'eighties like *Ben Hur* and *Way Down East*. There are two Frenchmen in the play, Ferdinand and Henry, who take their part in Maquis activity. They are good. Denise, Henry's wife, is bad because she wants her husband to join the Vichy militia so that she will not have to work any more. Her work apparently consists of shelling peas, for she soliloquizes over her fate:

> He won't join the army and if he did he would
> earn enough and I would only have to shell his

peas and my peas, not everybody's peas. Oh it is just too miserable of him.

As in the Victorian melodramas there are no nuances to this little play, no character development. The love scenes are incredible. It is obviously a juvenile performance. That fact brings one again to the core of Gertrude Stein. What is implicit in all her writings is her insistence on reacting as a child. In the plays and portraits it is the infantile repetitions, the echoes of counting-out rhymes, the stringing of words together the way a four-year-old strings wooden beads. In her autobiographies and war reflections the style and thought currents and general attitude are those of a wide-eyed child. Her inspiration turned back, not like Proust's to remembered childhood but to childhood itself. From what one can gather her views of American history, particularly about the Civil War, were still those of her schooldays. Her retreat into the atmosphere of childhood finally reached the extreme form of her *First Reader* where she tried to re-create the very form of the nineteenth-century McGuffey Readers. It is this stance that accounts for her genial and uncritical egotism, the natural egotism of the child who is the centre of his own solar system.

Gertrude Stein's rejection of the adult world that began tentatively with *Three Lives* became enforced in the automatism of her middle period and externally apparent in her autobiographies, was—however consciously motivated—a necessity to her. In her maturity she could apparently not manage or organize her world except on a juvenile level. She was the child that brooked no contradictions. Whereas there was another calculating side of her nature that could assess the publicity value of her position, it was an inner need that made her retreat into the shell of childhood, maintaining all the time in this retreat that she was one of the great figures of the age.

That she should have found recognition for her claims among her contemporaries was only possible because of the general intellectual climate, another aspect of the twentieth-century loss of nerve. Writing in *Time and Western Man* about the prevalence of this child-cult, Wyndham Lewis has traced the impulse to 'the terrible and generally hidden disturbances that have broken the back of our will in the Western countries, and have already forced us into the greatest catastrophes'. It is an escape impulse that can be seen in the dadaist longing for the lunatic asylum, in the sub-cerebral preoccupations of the surrealists, in the shadow-play of the German expressionists, in all the ephemeral movements that had as their one binding quality the retreat from reason.

Gertrude Stein carried this retreat back to the point where a child first becomes aware of words and sits mouthing them over and over again as if tasting their quality, unaware of the meaning but delighting in the process. Beyond that stage lies a wordless silence, as the Greek philosopher Cratylus discovered twenty-four hundred years before, when he became so obsessed with the relativity of words that according to Aristotle 'he finally did not think it right to say anything but only moved his finger'. Gertrude Stein reached her own silence, her final goal in Père-Lachaise, shortly before the publication of the *First Reader*.

ACKNOWLEDGEMENTS

Permission to use selections from copyrighted material has been given by the courtesy of the following authors, publishers and magazines, to whom grateful acknowledgement is made.

MESSRS. ALLEN, W. H., & CO., and MR. EDMUND WILSON: *The Wound and The Bow*, by Edmund Wilson, copyright by W. H. Allen & Co., and Messrs. Houghton Mifflin. (1941).

AMERICAN BOOK CO.: *A Short History of Greek Literature*, by Wilmer Cave Wright. Copyright 1907 by the American Book Co.

MESSRS. CAPE, JONATHAN, LTD.: *Exiles*, by James Joyce. Copyright 1936 by Jonathan Cape Ltd., and Messrs. Viking Co. *A Portrait of The Artist as a Young Man*. Copyright 1926 by Jonathan Cape Ltd., and Random House.

MESSRS. CHATTO & WINDUS LTD., and WYNDHAM LEWIS: *Time and Western Man*, by Wyndham Lewis. Copyright 1927.

MESSRS. CONSTABLE & CO. LTD.: *Convention and Revolt in Poetry*, by John Livingstone Lowes. Copyright 1919 by Constable & Co. Ltd., and Messrs. Houghton Mifflin Ltd.

CROWN PUBLISHERS: *Journey into the Self*, by Leo Stein—book, letters, papers and journals of Leo Stein, edited by Edmund Fuller. Copyright 1950 by The Estate of Leo Stein.

MESSRS. DENT, J. M., & SONS: *The Confident Years*, 1885-1915, by Van Wyck Brooks. Copyright 1952 by J. M. Dent & Sons and Messrs. E. F. Dutton.

THE EXPOSITION PRESS: *Gertrude Stein: Form and Intelligibility*, by R. S. Miller. Copyright 1949 by The Exposition Press.

MESSRS. FABER & FABER LTD.: *Finnegans Wake*, by James Joyce. Copyright 1939 by Faber & Faber Ltd., and The Executors of James Joyce. *James Joyce*, by Harry Levin. Copyright 1941 by Faber & Faber Ltd., and New Directions. *James Joyce's 'Ulysses'*, by Stuart Gilbert. Copyright 1930 by Faber & Faber Ltd., and Alfred A. Knopf. *A Skeleton Key to Finnegans Wake*, by Joseph Campbell and Henry Morton Robinson. Copyright 1947 by Faber & Faber, and Messrs. Harcourt, Brace (1944).

MESSRS. FARRER & RHINEHART: *James Joyce*, by Herbert Gorman. Copyright 1939 by Farrer & Rhinehart.

MESSRS. HARCOURT, BRACE & CO.: *The Autobiography of Alice B. Toklas*, by Gertrude Stein. Copyright 1933 by Harcourt, Brace & Co. *The Making of Americans*, by Gertrude Stein. Copyright 1934 by Harcourt, Brace & Co. *European Experiences*, by Mabel Dodge Luhan. Copyright 1935 by Harcourt, Brace & Co. *A Victorian in the Modern World*, by Powers Hapgood.

DATE DUE